A Passionate Mind
in Relentless Pursuit

ALSO BY NOLIWE ROOKS

Cutting School:
Privatization, Segregation, and the End of Public Education

Black fashion:
Art. Pleasure. Politics.

Women's Magazines and New Media (ed.)

White Money / Black Power:
The Surprising History of African American Studies
and the Crisis of Race in Higher Education

Ladies' Pages:
African American Women's Magazines
and the Culture That Made Them

Hair Raising:
Beauty, Culture, and African American Women

SIGNIFICATIONS

Series editor
Henry Louis Gates, Jr.

A Passionate Mind in Relentless Pursuit

———

THE VISION OF MARY MCLEOD BETHUNE

NOLIWE ROOKS

PENGUIN PRESS   NEW YORK   2024

PENGUIN PRESS
An imprint of Penguin Random House LLC
penguinrandomhouse.com

Grateful acknowledgment is made to Ebony Media Group, LLC,
for permission to reprint "My Last Will and Testament"
by Mary McLeod Bethune, *Ebony* magazine (1955).

LIBRARY OF CONGRESS CATALOGING-IN-PUBLICATION DATA
Names: Rooks, Noliwe, 1963– author.
Title: A passionate mind in relentless pursuit:
the vision of Mary McLeod Bethune / Noliwe Rooks.
Other titles: Vision of Mary McLeod Bethune
Description: New York: Penguin Press, 2024. | Series: Significations |
Includes bibliographical references and index.
Identifiers: LCCN 2023038347 (print) | LCCN 2023038348 (ebook) |
ISBN 9780593492420 (hardcover) | ISBN 9780593492437 (ebook)
Subjects: LCSH: Bethune, Mary McLeod, 1875–1955. |
African American women political activists—Biography. |
African Americans—Politics and government—20th century. |
African American women social reformers—Biography. |
African American women educators—Biography. |
Roosevelt, Eleanor, 1884–1962—Friends and associates. |
African Americans—Civil rights—History—20th century. |
Social change—United States—History—20th century
Classification: LCC E185.97.B34 R665 2024 (print) | LCC E185.97.B34 (ebook) |
DDC 370.92 [B]—dc23/eng/20240327
LC record available at https://lccn.loc.gov/2023038347
LC ebook record available at https://lccn.loc.gov/2023038348

Printed in the United States of America
1st Printing

Book design and Significations symbol by Daniel Lagin

For my mother, Belvie Jean Rooks

In all the ways you know,
and that I took too long to understand,
there would be no me without you

CONTENTS

A Passionate Mind
in Relentless Pursuit

1

"MY NAME IS MRS. BETHUNE"

In November 1938, Bull Connor, the commissioner of Public Safety in Birmingham, Alabama, and an ardent segregationist, threatened to arrest Eleanor Roosevelt for sitting with Black people in public. What set Bull Connor, the first lady, and twelve hundred bystanders on a collision course was the inaugural meeting of the Southern Conference for Human Welfare, a group formed to discuss how Alabama and the rest of the South could reduce poverty, improve the equitable enforcement of civil and constitutional rights, make credit and banking more widely available across racial lines, improve public education, reform the sharecropping/farm tenancy system, and embrace democracy by repealing the poll tax. For many who thought things in the South were fine as they were, with Black people disenfranchised, undereducated, and overtaxed, these goals were controversial and led to charges in the local press that the conference was a front for socialists and communist sympathizers. But more than fear about the group's political agenda, the cries of "race mixing" garnered the lion's share of public and media attention. Newspaper articles reported that members of the city's Ku Klux Klan had found a woman who represented white women Democrats and was coming forward to warn everyone that the gathering was a ruse to allow Black men and white women to engage in sex with one another.

Sociologist and Fisk University president Charles Johnson reported that the attendees were a "curiously mixed body which included labor leaders and economists, farmers and sharecroppers, industrialists and social executives, government officials and civic leaders, ministers and politicians, students and interested individuals." There was one thing they had in common: they all knew that on the morning of the second day of the conference, Eleanor Roosevelt would be joining the proceedings. However, few were prepared for the sight that greeted them that morning: the entire Birmingham police department out in force at the conference center with the exterior of the auditorium encircled by police cars, wagons, and motorcycles. And inside, policemen stood or leaned against every wall. Bull Connor grabbed a bullhorn and announced that anyone who failed to "segregate apart" would face immediate arrest. The attendees obeyed, sorting themselves with Black people on one side of the auditorium and white people on the other. That is where things stood when Eleanor Roosevelt arrived with Mary McLeod Bethune by her side. Ignoring the police officers who tried to steer her to the white section, the first lady joined Bethune on the "Black" side of the room. A moment after they settled themselves, one of the policemen tapped Roosevelt on the shoulder and told her to move or face arrest. Instead of acquiescing, she produced a folding chair, placed it in the aisle between the white and Black sections, and declared she would not move again, saying, "I refuse to be segregated."[1]

If you ever research Bethune's life, if you go looking for her in archives and oral histories, you will find that this recounting of Bethune and Eleanor Roosevelt arriving at the conference that day is an oft-told tale. I had seen the story about Eleanor Roosevelt defying Bull Connor, risking arrest, and challenging Birmingham's racial segregation laws so often that I had started to skim the words when some aspect of the event was mentioned. I found articles about the altercation in both the Black and the white press. I saw it in archives and in transcripts of audio recordings of speeches, and cited in biographical sources. Accounts always mention Eleanor Roosevelt, the first lady of the United

States, and only passingly mention Mary McLeod Bethune, whom Black people at the time referred to as the "first lady of the struggle" or the "first lady of Black America." Sometimes, Bethune is not mentioned at all. Roosevelt is always the focus, and Bethune's presence is something akin to smoke rising to signal a recently extinguished fire. She is present, seen, undeniably there, but understood as the result or aftermath of something more notable having taken place. That's why I was so surprised when I came across an interview with the conference's organizer, Virginia Durr, who shared what had happened the evening before the police and the first lady arrived. Mrs. Bethune provoked an incident that set the conference attendees abuzz simply by rising and saying her name. Durr described the impact, on the first evening of the conference, of attendees being able to sit where they pleased. "It was thrilling; it was really marvelous. The new day had come; the whole South was coming together to make a new day, and it was just thrilling." She recalled,

> The only thing I remember that happened particularly Sunday night was that Mrs. Louise Charlton, who had been one of the organizers . . . called on Mrs. Mary McLeod Bethune, and she called her Mary; she said, Mary, do you wish to come to the platform? And Mrs. Bethune got up . . . and she said, my name is Mrs. Bethune. So,

Louise Charlton had to say Mrs. Bethune, will you come to the platform. Well, that sounds like a small thing now, but that was a big dividing line. A Negro woman in Birmingham, Alabama, called Mrs. Bethune at a public meeting.[2]

When she stood, filled her lungs, and exhaled the word *Bethune* in the alto tone and deliberate cadence that enthralled audiences, she announced that something new and distinct was possible, as clearly as if she had woven those exact words into sentences. She confirmed what all must surely have known, that erasing the color line involved more than where and with whom they sat but included calling a Black woman by the name to which she chose to answer. Mary, the name used to summon her to the podium, might be any number of people, but at that time, in that moment, there was only one Mrs. Bethune. A Black woman born poor and raised in the Jim Crow South, who had spent at least a decade at that point also working with government officials and wealthy philanthropists "up south" in the North, she well knew that publicly correcting a white woman risked more than rebuke; she understood that it could invite physical or economic harm. But she also knew her name and she had every reason to believe others knew it too.

By the time Mrs. Bethune rose and made clear how she

should be addressed, she had spent the past decade providing her expertise to three US presidents. Her path to a seat at the national public policy table began in 1927 when Bethune attended a lunch hosted by Eleanor Roosevelt, the wife of Franklin Delano Roosevelt, who a year later would be elected governor of New York. When the white women in attendance, unused to socializing with Black people, refused to be seated with Bethune, Roosevelt placed Bethune beside her and invited any who objected to the seating arrangements to feel free to leave. The two developed a close friendship and political partnership that lasted through Eleanor's moving into the governor's mansion and later becoming the first lady.

Roosevelt advocated for Bethune to become an adviser to presidents, and the first knock on her door came in 1928, when Calvin Coolidge named her a delegate to a conference addressing child welfare in Washington, DC. Again, she was the only Black person invited to take part. That opportunity led to others. A year later, in 1929, Herbert Hoover asked her to serve on the National Commission for Child Welfare. In that role, she helped to design national surveys on health conditions, infant mortality, and public health programs. The results led to the establishment of the short-lived Child Health Day, programs to professionalize training for midwives, the passage of child labor laws, and vaccination programs to eliminate smallpox and diphtheria. In 1936, President Franklin Delano Roosevelt appointed her to the National Youth Administration (NYA), a federal agency created as part of the Depression-era Works Progress Administration (WPA). NYA programs funneled federal Depression-era relief money, training, programs, and employment opportunities to young people between the ages of sixteen and twenty-five. Bethune lobbied the agency so aggressively and effectively to attend to the needs of Black people who met the qualifications that she earned a full-time staff position in 1938. When she rose to speak at the Birmingham conference, it was as the director of the Division of Negro Affairs. In that role, she was the first Black person ever to head a federal division and at the time was the highest-paid Black person to have worked for the US government. There is also a real argument to be made that through her various roles in the Roosevelt administration, she had an impact in shifting the Black vote from one that had been reliably assumed by Republicans, given that Abraham Lincoln had been a Republican, to a bulwark for the Democratic Party, a shift that had culminated a few years before with the 1936 presidential election.

Finally, she was also able to use her access to the highest reaches of government to advocate for and form a coalition of leaders comprised of Black employees of the federal government. They were called the Federal Council of Negro Affairs. It came to be known as the Black Cabinet and served as an informal advisory board to the Roosevelt administration on issues facing Black people in the United States. Whenever the Black Cabinet gathered to meet, they did so either in Bethune's Capitol Hill office or in the living room of her home. She was a woman of drive, impact, and acclaim who at different stages of her life wielded an unusual amount of power. This last might explain why it is so easy to find instances where her friends, biographers, and colleagues describe her as arrogant, plain, dictatorial, unattractive, fat, and difficult. One of the Black Cabinet members, Robert Weaver, said she had the "marvelous gift of effecting feminine helplessness in order to attain her aims with masculine ruthlessness."[3]

When I first read Weaver's opinion of Bethune and tried to turn and twist it as one does when puzzling over the missing pieces needed to create a recognizable border framing a completed life, one of her accomplishments that came to mind involved her role in founding the World War II–era all-Black air force unit, the Tuskegee Airmen. She began work toward this goal in 1938 as a way to include Black colleges and universities in FDR's newly instituted Civilian Pilot Training Program, an initiative to ensure the nation had enough pilots in the event of war. The program was funded in part by the NYA and, fortuitously, Bethune headed its "Negro Section." She was determined not only to include Black colleges in the initiative but to use the whole as an opportunity to pursue integrating the nation's military. She also planned to have Black women serve as nurses who could provide medical and psychological counseling and support to the Black male pilots. She could clearly see that Black colleges sorely needed the money that came along with the program, Black people needed the military pay and benefits it offered, and Black women needed the opportunity to train for careers in nursing. As soon as the program was announced, she began lobbying President Roosevelt, urging him to extend the opportunity to Black colleges and Black people and to resist the perspective of the southern wing of the Democratic Party, who were ardent segregationists and did not want the military integrated or the federal government to offer Black people any type of training for which the federal government would pay.

Bethune prevailed and was soon able to get Tuskegee Institute, Hampton University, Virginia State, North Carolina A&T State, Delaware State, West Virginia State, and Howard University included among the colleges and universities participating in the federally funded Civilian Pilot Training Program. West Virginia State College became the first Black school to receive a military airplane in 1939. The Tuskegee Institute received its authorization and plane a few months later, in October of that same year. This was necessary forward movement but not enough to guarantee President Roosevelt would authorize the pilots to become a recognized military unit prepared to fight when required. Up until that point, most Black people in the military served in roles that were administrative or janitorial, or involved food service. They certainly did not fly planes. Bethune continued to strategize and soon devised a plan requiring the participation of her friend and ally of over a decade, Eleanor Roosevelt.[4]

Roosevelt and Bethune together paid a visit to the Tuskegee Institute's Moton Field in 1941 and, despite objections from her Secret Service detail, the first lady asked the chief flight instructor and Tuskegee pilot Charles Anderson if he would take her up in a plane. In what was likely the first time a Black pilot flew alone in the South with a white woman, Roosevelt spent more than an hour flying around in the skies over Tuskegee. Once back on the ground and in Washington, Roosevelt and Bethune used the success of the flight to continue to entreat the president to integrate the military and allow the pilots to fly. In December 1942, the president issued Executive Order 9279 ending segregation in the military. It never became law. The military remained segregated until 1948, though. The pilots trained at Black colleges became the first squadron of Black pilots to fly in World War II. I have a great-uncle, Virgil Richardson, who was a Tuskegee Airman. I grew up knowing that about him, but I did not know until researching Bethune's life that she was a large part of the reason he had the opportunity to soar. [5]

Mrs. Bethune is generally remembered today as an educator. It is true that she believed deeply in the power of education; she owed a large debt to how it had shaped her life from the age of twelve, when she became the first in her family to sit in a classroom. But education is just part of her story. She was a woman of "firsts." The fifteenth of seventeen children born to her parents in Maysville, South Carolina, she was the first born free, not as enslaved property. She was the first Black woman to establish a historically Black college for Black girls in the eastern part of the United States. Bethune was also the first to found a hospital for Black people in the state of Florida. Her "firsts" are a song of Black survival and safety. Her life was a multipart composition that climbed octaves and harmonized the individual, the cultural, the political, and the economic. She was a political theorist and visionary, a pragmatist who shape-shifted, a woman of consequence who strategized how the federal government, voting rights, Black capitalism, economic development, Black organizations, and Black segregation could sustain Black men, women, children, and old people during the hand-to-hand combat phase of the Black freedom struggle that was the Jim Crow era. She was clear-sighted and truth-speaking about the evils of segregation and the South's desire for it. In the late 1920s she argued that the commitment to Black inferiority was stubbornly in defiance of the basic tenets of capitalism:

> The South has definitely committed itself to the task of keeping the Negro in his place. That place by all accepted teaching and belief is and must be for all time an inferior one. To keep [Negroes] inferior they must be huddled in segregated ghettoes without drainage, light, pavement, or modern sanitary convenience. They must be denied justice and the right to make a decent living. They must be insulted and bullied and mobbed, discriminated against in public places and denied access to parks and recreational centers. In dollars and cents, the cost of this system is tremendous to the Commonwealth which sponsors it.[6]

Between the 1920s and the rise of the modern civil rights movement, which includes the Montgomery Bus Boycott of 1955 that made a young preacher named Martin Luther King, Jr., a household name and, later that same year, the murderous mutilation of Emmett Till, there were few political strategies, organizations, or institutions aimed at aiding the survival and advancement of Black people that did not bear the imprint of Bethune's involvement, sometimes felt as a five-fingered handprint as it slapped white supremacy full in the face, sometimes more like the felt yet unseen trace of a fingertip's caress.

Historian Deborah Gray White has said that, in terms of the political ideologies and strategies Black women embraced in the twentieth century, Bethune "was a transitional figure whose political ideology was grounded in the nineteenth-century belief that advancement would come through changing individual behavior." As she gained more experience and arguably grew more confident in her own thinking, Bethune began to see that any organization saying it wanted to bene-fit the largest number of Black people had to forgo the relent-less focus on changing individual attitudes and behaviors and eschew the debilitating focus on being "respectable" and include "changing social, economic, and political insti-tutions that shaped collective opinions." The first pillars up-holding an inclusive democracy that she wanted to shore up and reposition to include Black people were voting and edu-cation. She understood that the ballot and the book were powerful and necessary tools capable of keeping Black peo-ple safe as they forged a path toward freedom in the United States. She knew both were threats to the status quo, if for no other reason than she so often found whites willing to engage in intimidating if not terroristic behavior to keep Black people from having either. Over time, she developed, sharpened, and implemented a multipronged plan to safeguard and advance a comprehensive strategy for emancipation in a world where both voting and education were very necessary but could not possibly be everything. Bethune could clearly see that if these two were the only tools in the Black freedom toolbox, destroying schools and disrupting access to the ballot box could derail an entire agenda.[7]

This was an insight born of hard personal experience in Florida, where the political reality illustrated, even to the casual observer, that Black people's theoretical right to vote or attend school and their actual access to the ballot box or classroom were two entirely separate things. Specific to voting, for Black people, state and municipal ordinances presented any number of "legal" obstacles as they trod along the road to a voting booth and the promised protections of enfranchisement, keeping most Black people from voting by a variety of measures, including insisting that only voters whose grandfathers had historically had the right to vote could cast their ballots. Such a high percentage of Black people had grandparents who were enslaved, and so of course legally denied the right to vote, that this provision effectively disenfranchised the majority. Some towns required Black voters to wait in line all day and into the evening to vote, allowing them to enter the polling place only after all white people had concluded the exercise of their constitutional right. Leaving one's place in line to use the restroom, get a bite to eat, or go in search of a cool drink of water would ensure that, if they were Black, they could not vote that day. In this context, Bethune understood political strategies that homed in on style and personal comportment, or ones that put all faith in the ballot box, to be naive. She knew she would need to organize and found organizations to begin putting her larger ambitions in place.

There are stories in these pages about how Bethune moved the needle on voting rights, included Black people in federal initiatives, brought about regulations governing child labor, and advanced a variety of programs to protect the health of children and pregnant women. She expanded educational opportunities for Black people, lobbied for the inclusion of Black people in the military, conjured the idea of the Tuskegee Airmen, and then endeavored to make them a reality. She served as president, vice president, or founder in a variety of civil rights and mutual aid organizations, including the National Association for the Advancement of Colored People (NAACP), the Urban League, the Association for the Study of African American Life and History (ASALH), the United Negro College Fund (UNCF), the National Association of Colored Women's Clubs (NACWC), and the National Council of Negro Women (NCNW). Her tools were her voice, her courage, her faith, her intellect, and her ability to inspire others to join her in keeping their eyes upturned toward a distant horizon where democratic peaks would one day come into view.

Those qualities help explain what rooted her, her students, and the faculty of her Daytona girls' school in place when the Ku Klux Klan showed up, torches blazing, hoods affixed firmly on heads, to intimidate them. The standoff occurred in 1920, in the months following the passage of the Nineteenth Amendment giving women the right to the vote. In the run-up to the first election following its passage, Bethune went door-to-door organizing the community and raising donations to pay the "poll tax" for Black voters. This tax was a controversial but legal fee to suppress Black voting since many Black people did not have an extra dollar with which to part. Bethune would tell those hesitant about paying to vote, or about threats from the Klan,

Eat your bread without butter but pay your poll tax! Nobody ever told me to pay my poll tax. My dollar is always there on time. Do not be afraid of the Klan. Quit running. Hold your head up high. Look every man straight in the eye and make no apology to anyone because of race or color. When you see a burning cross remember the Son of God who bore the heaviest.[8]

Another barrier to voting in Florida and elsewhere was literacy tests. Election officials demanded that Black people read aloud from materials such as the Constitution of the United States to vote. In response to officials putting this law on the books, Bethune conducted night classes to teach reading for free to any who wished to learn. These classes, obviously aimed at expanding voting access, attracted negative attention from members of the white community who did not believe Black people should be allowed to vote and were not particularly enthusiastic about their learning how to read. One evening, representatives of the Ku Klux Klan sent word that if she didn't stop what she was doing, teaching reading and baking cakes and pies to raise money to pay community poll taxes, they would come to her Daytona school for girls and burn it to the ground. They said they might not stop with buildings but might also harm her or her students. The night of their promised arrival, Klan members contacted sympathetic city officials and asked them to turn off all the streetlamps in the town of Daytona. They asked them to do it just as night fell. In the deepening dusk, eighty or so Klan members rode on horseback through the streets in full white-supremacist regalia, the only illumination visible to riders or watchers the orange-tinted flicker of their burn-ing torches, the only sound the beat of hooves coming near.

While city officials had extinguished the lights in town, on campus where she was in charge, Bethune fought the dark with light. As the Klan caravan approached, she instructed the staff to turn on every light on the grounds and in all the school buildings. When the Klan entered the gates of the school, they found it illuminated and could well see Bethune standing straight as she faced them. Secreted out of view were a number of Black men from the community who had armed themselves and were prepared to do bloody battle to defend the school, the students, and Bethune, but Klan members couldn't see them. What they did see was their group of 80 dwarfed by the 150 students, staff, and teachers who stood beside Bethune, singing to one another not to be afraid because "God Will Take Care of You." Whether it was the unexpected presence of light on campus, the Lord, the numbers of women and girls standing, singing, afraid but committed to their right to be, there was no violence that night. The white supremacists merely rode in one gate of the school and out the other. They never even slowed down.

If their goal was intimidation, it did not work. The next morning, Bethune led a procession of 100 Black women to the polls to vote for the first time. Though they had arrived early, poll workers forced them to wait outside in long, winding lines. As usual, they were told that any who left the line for any reason would be denied the right to vote. Bethune, when recounting the scene, always ended with "but we voted."[9] Bethune's resolve was no small thing. Florida had the highest lynching rate in the country, and more than 260 Black Floridians died in this manner between 1882 and 1930. The Klan visited Bethune's school on other occasions. She, her students, and her school remained unharmed. When the story of her defiance of the KKK spread, Bethune began to field requests to speak to audiences about rights, race, and democracy. Her star was just beginning to shine.[10]

Though she is not primarily remembered as a businesswoman, over the course of her life, Bethune invested in numerous businesses, including *The Pittsburgh Courier*, where she had a column, and in a handful of primarily Black-serving life insurance companies, including the Central Life Insurance of Florida, which she cofounded. She also helped family members open far-flung businesses such as at least one family mortuary business and at least one beauty salon. Near the end of her life, she founded a beach about forty-five minutes from Daytona, both for Black people to have the chance to own beachfront property and just to provide recreational opportunities for Black people, who were barred even from swimming on most of Florida's beaches. The idea to start a beach for Black people in Florida was not new or unique.

Bethune had been deeply involved in founding another beach, named American Beach, a few hours north of Daytona. However, the idea for this one was said to have come out of several incidents in the early 1940s when Bethune tried to take some of her students to Daytona Beach and white citizens and police officers quickly ordered them off, forbidding them from swimming. In short order, Bethune rounded up a list of investors, including local business owners and the presidents of two insurance companies. They put together $113,000 and bought land stretching for about 2.5 miles, dividing it into 2,547 lots. It was later named Bethune Beach. Its charter forbade white people from owning property there. It was to be a beach for Black people.[11]

Near the end of her life, Mary McLeod Bethune was the lone Black woman appointed as a member of the United States delegation to the 1945 conference in San Francisco to draft the United Nations charter. She had to work for the invitation. President Roosevelt had died, Eleanor was no longer first lady, and the new president, Harry Truman, did not think Bethune needed to attend. She called upon the former first lady for help and Roosevelt again answered the call, interceding on Bethune's behalf with the new president. Part of what motivated Bethune's interest in the conference was the fact that she had begun to see similarities between the struggles of Black people in the United States and move-ments for independence in other countries, especially in Africa and Asia. She wanted to attend and urge the body to acknowledge the links between the white supremacy of Jim Crow segregation and the colonialism that impeded the freedom dreams of people in Asia, Africa, and elsewhere. Writing about her impressions of the gathering, Bethune noted that she was happy to see groups of Black people repre-senting political, religious, and fraternal organizations gath-ered outside the San Francisco meeting to advocate for their positions and to link their vision of peace and freedom with that of many millions of other people around the world. She wrote: "Through this Conference the Negro becomes closely allied with the darker races of the world, but more impor-tantly he becomes integrated into the structure of the peace and freedom of all people everywhere." She saw the gather-ing as an opportunity to lobby attendees from around the world on the importance of ending colonialism, securing an international bill of rights, and prioritizing education and culture in the UN's work.[12]

Those are the things Bethune did. But to feel her impact, to understand her genius, is a more subtle matter. It is not always so easy to see her contributions, to find her amid the more powerful with whom she interacted. Just as an exhalation of warm breath on cold glass produces mist that endures long enough to write a name before it fades, Bethune's breath warmed the cold, clear glass that was the white supremacist status quo between the 1920s and the midcentury civil rights movement. She wrote her name there. With the passage of time, her signature has faded. The ways Bethune appears, disappears, pushes forward, falls back in the politics and culture of the age in which she lived reminds me of the fog I grew up with on a hill in San Francisco named Potrero. As a resident of that place, I had an intimate relationship with fog. Those of us who grew up in fog know it is water gifting air with substance. It is air and water determined to attract notice as both are transformed. I have felt its approach when it was still "barely there" translucent, and bundled myself against it when it was so thick that it was hard to hold on to a confident sense of place, time, or the best way forward. In San Francisco, fog moves west to east, rushing from the Pacific Ocean and across the city to San Francisco Bay. The view from our living room was of Twin Peaks, the two western hills five miles away. When I was a child, fog would hide behind those peaks and then spill toward me as it tumbled down to the valley between, before drawing itself back up and out to the sea. Sometimes, fog would come all the way over to my hill, wrapping the world with a not quite gray haze that rendered the most familiar views of the yard, neighbor's house, or light poles unrecognizable and mysterious. Growing up watching fog creep, I understood that it is always a good idea to keep at least one eye on developments just over the horizon. If protection from the elements is required, it is best to know about it early enough to be prepared with an extra layer of outerwear and a heightened level of resolve about the trip. If a change in direction is warranted so that the road you travel will remain visible, it is good to know ahead of time. To grow up knowing fog is to understand that it is impossible to make successful plans about the future without understanding what is approaching—its essence and nature. Seeing fog approach teaches you to think about what will be required for you and yours to remain safe and unbothered.

I am asking you to think about air and water and hills and fog because, for me, writing this book became a process of understanding that in order to find and see Bethune, I would have to navigate the research and writing in ways similar to how I learned to drive in fog. If I was going to safely reach my destination, I had to focus hard on what I could see right in front of me, go as slowly as circumstances would allow, and lower the illumination of my headlights so I could see enough of the road to keep creeping productively forward. Both fog and Bethune forced me to look out at a world I thought I knew well and see it as re-formed and transformed.

Researching and writing this book also reminded me that in fog, it is easier to see peaks than valleys. As fog over-fills valleys, making them dense, hazy, and cold, the only way to get your bearings, reorient yourself to your exact location, is to tilt your neck back, search the distance, and find a peak. I see the year of Bethune's birth in 1875, two years before the end of the era known as Reconstruction in 1877, as a peak, a high-water mark of multiracial democracy in the United States. It was a period of demonstrated commitment at the federal level to making sure Black people in the South, where more than 90 percent of them lived, could vote, have an education provided by public tax dollars, own land unmolested, know citizenship. Union troops protected Black lives and citizenship rights during Reconstruction, but it didn't last long. By the time Bethune arrived in the world, democracy had begun to recede and the fog of authoritarianism in the South, having been pushed out to sea for a bit, gathered, reversed course, and crept back toward shore. Bethune died in May 1955, less than a year before the Montgomery Bus Boycott began and just a few months before Emmett Till's murder became another spark igniting the modern civil rights movement, with its focus on once again delivering enfranchisement, citizenship, protection, and a challenge to the segregationist color line. In each decade between 1904, when she founded her girls' school, and 1955, when she died, Bethune moved through the political landscape by feel, maneuvered by faith, peered with lifted eyes through the gauzy dark, always searching for the peak that would lead her to the high ground of freedom. Always a strategist, as she prepared for the freedom she was sure would come, Bethune studied the horizon line, saw what was what, and prepared for the return of the fog of fascism, disenfranchisement, violence, and economic exploitation. Bethune knew this fog. She studied it. She learned how to move with and through it. She understood the layers of inner resolve and outer comportment she would need to don and discard, depending on how thick or light were the conditions. It was a dance, the steps of which she spent her life trying to teach to others.

On May 18, 1955, Bethune died of a heart attack at her adopted and long-term home in Daytona, Florida. As befitting someone who had contributed as much as she had to the United States and, indeed, the world, her passing led to an outpouring of condolences, remembrances, and testimonials. For weeks, tributes popped up in Black newspapers across the United States. In the Introduction to the *Bethune Papers*, scholar Elaine Smith offers a sampling of the notice Bethune's death attracted. She says that the Oklahoma City *Black Dispatch* ran an editorial describing her as "Exhibit

No. 1 for all who have faith in America and the democratic process." The *Atlanta Daily World* described the arc of her life as having been "one of the most dramatic careers ever enacted at any time upon the stage of human activity." A writer in *The Pittsburgh Courier*, a paper in which Bethune owned stock, wrote, "In any race or nation she would have been an outstanding personality and made a noteworthy contribution because her chief attribute was her indomitable soul." Smith also notes the attention Bethune received from the white press, quoting the *Christian Century* as saying, "The story of her life should be taught to every school child for generations to come." *The New York Times* noted she was "one of the most potent factors in the growth of interracial goodwill in America." *The Washington Post* said, "So great were her dynamism and force that it was almost impossible to resist her. . . . Not only her own people, but all America has been enriched and ennobled by her courageous, ebullient spirit." Her hometown newspaper, the *Daytona Beach Evening News*, printed, "To some, she seemed unreal, something that could not be. . . . What right had she to greatness? . . . The lesson of Mrs. Bethune's life is that genius knows no racial barriers." Her star burned brightly upon her leaving this world.[13]

A few months before her death, Bethune wrote a document that she described as her last will and testament, which was not about material gifts but a meditation on the course of her life and her beliefs and principles. "My Last Will and Testament," published in *Ebony* magazine after she died, was meant to bequeath her accumulated wisdom and insight to future generations of Black people who she knew would continue to struggle for equality. There is no better introduction to this great soul's life and work than to read the text in her own words:

MARY MCLEOD BETHUNE'S
LAST WILL AND TESTAMENT

Sometimes as I sit communing in my study, I feel that death is not far off. I am aware that it will overtake me before the greatest of my dreams—full equality for the Negro in our time—is realized. Yet, I face that reality without fear or regrets. I am resigned to death as all humans must be at the proper time. Death neither alarms nor frightens one who has had a long career of fruitful toil. The knowledge that my work has been helpful to many fills me with joy and great satisfaction.

Since my retirement from an active role in educational work and from the affairs of the National Council of Negro Women, I have been living quietly and working at my desk at my home here in Florida. The years have directed a change of pace for me. I am now 78 years old and my activities are no longer so strenuous as they once were. I feel that I must conserve my strength to finish the work at hand.

Already I have begun working on my autobiography which will record my life-journey in detail, together with the innumerable side trips which have carried me abroad, into every corner of our country, into homes both lowly and luxurious, and even into the White House to confer with Presidents. I have also deeded my home and its contents to the Mary McLeod Bethune Foundation, organized in March, 1953, for research, interracial activity and the sponsorship of wider educational opportunities.

Sometimes I ask myself if I have any other legacy to leave. Truly, my worldly possessions are few. Yet, my experiences have been rich. From them, I have distilled principles and policies in which I believe firmly, for they represent the meaning of my life's work. They are the products of much sweat and sorrow.

Perhaps in them there is something of value. So, as my life draws to a close, I will pass them on to Negroes everywhere in the hope that an old woman's philosophy may give them inspiration. Here, then is my legacy.

I LEAVE YOU LOVE. Love builds. It is positive and helpful. It is more beneficial than hate. Injuries quickly forgotten quickly pass away. Personally, and racially, our enemies must be forgiven. Our aim must be to create a world of fellowship and justice where no man's skin, color or religion, is held against him. "Love thy neighbor" is a precept which could transform the world if it were universally practiced. It connotes brotherhood and, to me, brotherhood of man is the noblest concept in all human relations. Loving your neighbor means being interracial, interreligious and international.

I LEAVE YOU HOPE. The Negro's growth will be great in the years to come. Yesterday, our ancestors endured the degradation of slavery, yet they retained their dignity. Today, we direct our economic and political strength toward winning a more abundant and secure life. Tomorrow, a new Negro, unhindered by race taboos and shackles, will benefit from more than 330 years of ceaseless striving and struggle. Theirs will be a better world. This I believe with all my heart.

I LEAVE YOU THE CHALLENGE OF DEVELOPING CONFIDENCE IN ONE ANOTHER. As long as

Negroes are hemmed into racial blocks by prejudice and pressure, it will be necessary for them to band together for economic betterment. Negro banks, insurance companies and other businesses are examples of successful, racial economic enterprises. These institutions were made possible by vision and mutual aid. Confidence was vital in getting them started and keeping them going. Negroes have got to demonstrate still more confidence in each other in business. This kind of confidence will aid the economic rise of the race by bringing together the pennies and dollars of our people and ploughing them into useful channels. Economic separatism cannot be tolerated in this enlightened age, and it is not practicable. We must spread out as far and as fast as we can, but we must also help each other as we go.

I LEAVE YOU A THIRST FOR EDUCATION. Knowledge is the prime need of the hour. More and more, Negroes are taking full advantage of hard-won opportunities for learning, and the educational level of the Negro population is at its highest point in history. We are making greater use of the privileges inherent in living in a democracy. If we continue in this trend, we

will be able to rear increasing numbers of strong, pur-
poseful men and women, equipped with vision, mental
clarity, health and education.

I LEAVE YOU RESPECT FOR THE USES OF
POWER. We live in a world which respects power
above all things. Power, intelligently directed, can lead
to more freedom. Unwisely directed, it can be a dread-
ful, destructive force. During my lifetime I have seen
the power of the Negro grow enormously. It has always
been my first concern that this power should be placed
on the side of human justice.

Now that the barriers are crumbling everywhere, the
Negro in America must be ever vigilant lest his forces
be marshalled behind wrong causes and undemocratic
movements. He must not lend his support to any group
that seeks to subvert democracy. That is why we must
select leaders who are wise, courageous, and of great
moral stature and ability. We have great leaders among
us today: Ralph Bunche, Channing Tobias, Mordecai
Johnson, Walter White, and Mary Church Terrell.
[The latter now deceased]. We have had other great men
and women in the past: Frederick Douglass, Booker T.

Washington, Harriet Tubman, and Sojourner Truth. We must produce more qualified people like them, who will work not for themselves, but for others.

I LEAVE YOU FAITH. Faith is the first factor in a life devoted to service. Without faith, nothing is possible. With it, nothing is impossible. Faith in God is the greatest power, but great, too, is faith in oneself. In 50 years the faith of the American Negro in himself has grown immensely and is still increasing. The measure of our progress as a race is in precise relation to the depth of the faith in our people held by our leaders. Frederick Douglass, genius though he was, was spurred by a deep conviction that his people would heed his counsel and follow him to freedom. Our greatest Negro figures have been imbued with faith. Our forefathers struggled for liberty in conditions far more onerous than those we now face, but they never lost the faith. Their perseverance paid rich dividends. We must never forget their sufferings and their sacrifices, for they were the foundations of the progress of our people.

I LEAVE YOU RACIAL DIGNITY. I want Negroes to maintain their human dignity at all costs. We, as Negroes, must recognize that we are the custodians as well as the heirs of a great civilization. We have given something to the world as a race and for this we are proud and fully conscious of our place in the total picture of mankind's development. We must learn also to share and mix with all men. We must make an effort to be less race conscious and more conscious of individual and human values. I have never been sensitive about my complexion. My color has never destroyed my self-respect nor has it ever caused me to conduct myself in such a manner as to merit the disrespect of any person. I have not let my color handicap me. Despite many crushing burdens and handicaps, I have risen from the cotton fields of South Carolina to found a college, administer it during its years of growth, become a public servant in the government of our country and a leader of women. I would not exchange my color for all the wealth in the world, for had I been born white I might not have been able to do all that I have done or yet hope to do.

I LEAVE YOU A DESIRE TO LIVE HARMONI-OUSLY WITH YOUR FELLOW MEN. The problem of color is worldwide. It is found in Africa and Asia,

Europe and South America. I appeal to American Negroes—North, South, East and West—to recognize their common problems and unite to solve them.

I pray that we will learn to live harmoniously with the white race. So often, our difficulties have made us hypersensitive and truculent. I want to see my people conduct themselves naturally in all relationships—fully conscious of their manly responsibilities and deeply aware of their heritage. I want them to learn to understand whites and influence them for good, for it is advisable and sensible for us to do so. We are a minority of 15 million living side by side with a white majority. We must learn to deal with these people positively and on an individual basis.

I LEAVE YOU FINALLY A RESPONSIBILITY TO OUR YOUNG PEOPLE. The world around us really belongs to youth for youth will take over its future management. Our children must never lose their zeal for building a better world. They must not be discouraged from aspiring toward greatness, for they are to be the leaders of tomorrow. Nor must they forget that the masses of our people are still underprivileged, ill-housed, impoverished and victimized by discrimination. We have a powerful potential in our youth, and we must have the courage to change old ideas and practices so that we may direct their power toward good ends.

Faith, courage, brotherhood, dignity, ambition, responsibility—these are needed today as never before. We must cultivate them and use them as tools for our task of completing the establishment of equality for the Negro. We must sharpen these tools in the struggle that faces us and find new ways of using them. The Freedom Gates are half-ajar. We must pry them fully open.

If I have a legacy to leave my people, it is my philosophy of living and serving. As I face tomorrow, I am content, for I think I have spent my life well. I pray now that my philosophy may be helpful to those who share my vision of a world of Peace, Progress, Brotherhood, and Love.[14]

Bethune deserves a biopic, a multivolume biography, a theatrical production, a graphic novel, or a video game with AI immersion that will help to bring the pieces we know of her to life. I have been thinking about how her commitments to Black capital challenge ideas of Black capitalism as the surest way to help and support Black communities. I am intrigued by the lessons she has left us about how to organize with and for Black women in multiple ways and registers. I am delving more deeply into what the lesson of her life and symbol tells us about the tension between representation versus commemoration as the most potent political weapon, and how at the end of her life, she came to embrace peace as the only battle ultimately worth waging.

When I began researching this book, I knew my grandmother had graduated from Bethune-Cookman University and that my grandparents knew Bethune. But, if I am honest, I also thought of her as someone who might be considered to have been more an accommodationist to white power than an activist dedicating her life to banishing to hell any talk of Black inferiority. That is the first thing I came to understand I had gotten wrong. The other invaluable insight I learned came while poring over archival documents and microfilms as well as family records. I pieced together that my grandmother had graduated in 1947 from the school Bethune founded, the same year Bethune returned from her work in Washington, DC, to serve as the college's president once again. I felt and feel a special attachment and gratitude that she founded the school that allowed my grandmother to become a teacher. Teaching was my grandmother's dream and gave her life purpose. I also learned that my grandfather knew Bethune through his political work in the state of Florida and his work with the NAACP in the 1940s. I hadn't known about that when I found correspondence between them. Looking for Bethune, I found parts of my grandparents that allowed me to know them in a bigger, wider, more important context than I had before. I came to understand education as a starting point for Black empowerment and teachers as fighters who kept their students' eyes trained on collective safety and advancement. My grandparents and Bethune and the thousands of people she touched, worked with, inspired, and urged to build for freedom are not famous, remembered, much studied, or thought about in terms of political theory, intellectual history, or the struggle for Black freedom. They should be. They all should be. If for no other reason than to learn that truth, this is a book I needed to write, and Bethune's was a story I needed to find.

This is a book about how Bethune learned to step confidently through what I think of as the fog that engulfed her life and the lives of many of the people about whom she most cared. It is about what she learned of strategizing, organizing, freedom dreaming, and moving the torch of justice enough so that its glow illuminated, even if only a little bit, the path ahead. It is also a book about how she has helped me see home, both the places that I ate, slept, cried, and grinned in, and the larger nation encompassing it all. At some point while writing this book about Bethune, I came to know, feel, and understand that I was looking for the tools I needed to rebuild my literal and figurative understanding of "home." Looking for home, I found Bethune.

2

REMEMBERING BETHUNE

Because I spent summers and even school years living with my grandparents, my childhood was split between California and Florida. In Florida, I grew up in a house at 1139 Pierce Street in a Black community called the Heights. My grandparents built it in a town called Clearwater, in their home state. We all first made one another's acquaintance in 1963, three months after I was born. The house, my grandparents, and the community are all gone now. I think the journey to the house disappearing began the day the city decided to pave the road out front. I was about seven, and from my little-girl point of view, the smell of tar, the sight of orange-hatted men, and the grunting of construction equipment changed everything. That is when the house next door, the one that belonged to a slew of playmates, got picked up and moved somewhere else. The man who used to come by and rake and sweep the red dust of the road into submission was no longer needed, I guess, since I never saw him again once the hardened gray asphalt overtook everything. The boarded-up Black school that had stood for over a decade as a familiar neighborhood ruin vanished soon after too. One day the house on the corner where groups of Black men sat out on couches day in and out, talking, drinking, and playing cards, turned into an empty lot. The church up the street closed its doors, boarded its windows, and moved on to a new location. Then the house where a widower artfully hung what I would have called trash but others called "found art" from the branches of the trees outside his home vanished too. The small, neat houses occupied by the teachers and hairdressers and janitors and electricians and plumbers were gone, seemingly in the amount of time it takes a camera shutter's whir to click.

By the time we all learned that the ground underneath the whole community was something called a "Superfund" site—a place so polluted by manufacturing and chemicals that it was just not healthy for anyone to live on or grow vegetables—more houses and businesses disappeared. Finally, the killing blow came when the powers that be decided that though the nearest body of water, the Gulf of Mexico, was two miles away, the community would be taxed as waterfront property, as if it were all sitting on a white sand beach instead of landlocked and on polluted land. This decision tripled everyone's taxes in the time it took for the metaphorical ink to dry on the new proclamation. After a few years, 1139 Pierce Street was all that remained to remind anyone that there had ever been more than car lots and office buildings on that street and in the surrounding blocks. The house I grew up in stood lone and lonely for decades after most everyone and everything left. I asked my father once why he didn't sell it to one of the businesses that were always asking. He asked me, "Where would I go?" He died there. The house was dismantled soon after.

What I am saying is that though I fully understand that change comes in waves and stages, this wave and that stage came into view at the exact moment concrete replaced dirt in front of my grandparents' house. The mango tree that kept an entire neighborhood in shiny-mouthed, hand-dripping sweetness still blooms there. The thirty-foot-tall oak tree that I learned to climb (and once decided to test the limits of my bones by jumping from its highest branches—I do not actually recommend this) remains. But the once yellow then seafoam-green house whose address I don't remember not knowing is gone. I said goodbye to the occupants of that house over decades with tears, flowers, and ceremonies. I never planned or practiced how to process the finality of the

"I will never again see you in person" absent house. I will not forget it, but remembering home is more comforting, I think, when the structure stands. Otherwise, memory, regret, and fear whisper warnings about absence leading to forgetting or, worse still, to being forgotten. The danger in forgetting is not really about not being able to call up the image of one house. It is about the tragedy of those who will come after we are gone, never knowing that there was once a community that had been, struggled, withstood, succumbed, and tried to claim and make home a story of triumph, protection, and survival to be told to and passed down for them. To be honest, I don't think the structures end up mattering as much as what the intent and meaning of those who built and lived in the community have to teach us all about succor, if not survival. It's just easier to tell those stories when we have something to point at and hold on to as example and inspiration. Commemoration is a way to shine a guiding light through fog and darkness. It is meant to comfort, is an act akin to leaving bread crumbs for those we trust will come after and need a path, a little light, a little guidance on their road to naming and embracing their liberation. For people who are not free, do not know equity, only have the trust in a future to keep them going, commemoration is a way of saying someone lived here, someone died here, someone planned here, and your knowing them, your knowing what they did, your knowing who they are might one day bring comfort, urge a smile, or save a life.

This is part of how I think Bethune understood commemoration and I believe why she fought to make sure the buildings and homes that had housed Black people who were significant thinkers, actors, organizers, and doers were protected and remained. She wanted future generations to at least be able to find them, to follow. During her lifetime, the list of homes she sought to preserve, that she mentioned as needing care and attention, included theologian and religious scholar Howard Thurman's childhood home in Daytona, Florida; abolitionist writer and orator Frederick Douglass's home in Washington, DC; scholar, teacher, and founder of ASALH and Negro History Week Carter G. Woodson's home, also in DC; the headquarters of the National Association of Colored Women's Clubs; Council House, the headquarters of the National Council of Negro Women and Bethune's last home in DC; and finally, the house on the campus of Bethune-Cookman where Bethune lived most of her life and in which she died. Taken together, those houses and people represented pieces of a puzzle she spent most of her life trying to complete. She understood that the best way to hold tight to the dreams of a whole community was in fact to begin with the structures they built and paid for, and often in which they died.

When I drove past the Clearwater house and discovered it gone, I had just recently moved to Providence, Rhode Island. Providence is a city that is very much part of a region that believes in commemorating those who played a role in founding the United States, or the city, or the state. It is uncommon in the part of the city where I live and work to pass a stone structure and not see a marker affixed to its outside. Sometimes the writing on it is about the architect and the day the building was completed and why its style is important. Sometimes you learn about what had taken place inside. Sometimes you learn about the life of the occupant, like how John Brown, one of the founders of the university where I work, had amassed great wealth and position because of his lucrative career as "slave trader, profiteer, China trader, merchant and patriot." At the very least, strolling past this marker let you know someone of significance had lived there. Someone to honor, to loathe, to remember, to know. This message is harder to convey when the whole community and all the structures defining it are torn down and replaced.

Knowing this, I formed questions about Mary McLeod Bethune that I turned over and over with the concentration of pushing and rolling a lump of hard, sweet candy from tongue to cheek with a suck. Is Bethune so well commemorated because of the woman she was or as the symbol we want her to be? Can commemorating her be an act of committed devotion to building as high and tall a wall as possible to serve as a bulwark against forgetting? Is commemoration an opportunity to provide future generations with a direct path to their finding, entering, and rising from water baptized with clarity and purpose as they prepare for the struggle ahead? I believe the answers to these questions provide a shortcut to understanding why so many people across the country made sure that the towns she visited, places she lived, nation she served, honored her presence. Her reach and significance were so widespread that a journalist in her home state of South Carolina, on the occasion of Bethune's induction into the state's hall of fame, marveled, "If there was a Mount Rushmore for Black America, she would be on it." A former mayor of Daytona, her adopted hometown, declared, "Mary McLeod Bethune has an unrivaled place in our history. She is on Daytona Beach's Mount Rushmore." In the absence of an actual mountain into which to carve her likeness, installing statues and naming schools, roads, parks, beaches, and even housing projects after her has had to suffice.[1]

One example of her widespread popularity can be found in poet, writer, and activist Langston Hughes's 1956 autobiography, *I Wonder as I Wander.* There the writer recalled attending a reading with Bethune, his longtime advocate and mentor, at Bethune-Cookman College in 1929. After the event, Bethune asked if she might hitch a ride back to New York City with him. This was a ride requiring the duo to make their way up the Eastern Seaboard and through a good number of Jim Crow states where Black travelers could not count on being able to find hotels and restaurants willing to serve them. Hughes noted that Bethune avoided much of the indignity of segregated facilities along the long road to New York because "colored people along the eastern seaboard spread a feast and opened their homes wherever Mrs. Bethune passed their way." In fact, he continued, "chickens, sensing that she was coming, went flying off frantically seeking a hiding place. They knew a heaping platter of southern fried chicken would be made in her honor."[2]

Currently, there are two statues of Bethune on display in Washington, DC. The process of bringing both into being is about the devotion of a people who believed she championed something about who they were and what they needed to keep each other free as the past arced forward to skim the present and touch the future. Bethune meant something to Black people all over the nation. Their multigenerational commemorations of her sent a message that both celebrated the fact of democracy in the United States and lamented its fiction, and testified to the resilience of their dreams of citizenship.

The National Park Service has a document on its web-

site called the Mary McLeod Bethune Trail. It is a map of the
Eastern Seaboard on which there is a red line running from
south to north, a mostly straight line connecting the places it
manages and/or recommends that one visit. The trip starts in
Daytona, Florida, where Bethune founded Bethune-Cookman
University and McLeod Hospital and where her body lies
beneath a wind-nudged sway of moss. It continues to Maysville, South Carolina, where a marker proclaims the land on
which she was born is nearby, before it continues on up to
DC, where Council House, her home and the headquarters
of the National Council of Negro Women, is cared for by the
National Park Service. The trail ends in New York City at
the West 137th Street YWCA, where she held the first planning meeting to discuss forming the National Association of
Colored Women's Clubs.

Neither of the two statues of Bethune in Washington,
DC, is listed on the Bethune trail. They should be. One was
installed when Richard Nixon was president, on what would
have been her ninety-ninth birthday. The second was approved when Donald Trump held office but was installed
during the Biden-Harris administration, almost seventy
years after Bethune's heart attacked her and she died. In
both instances, grassroots movements rose up to support
and fund Bethune's having a statue, as a way to remind those
whose hope waned that organizing mattered and freedom

was a process. I believe commemoration is impactful when citizens tax, rally, and rouse themselves to make the demand. During Bethune's life, and in the aftermath when her legacy was solidified, who she was and what she believed mattered enough that there were always some willing to fight to ensure future generations would recognize her, know what she stood for, and see what she looked like as well.[3]

I think Bethune—her image, her statues, her name—may be a kind of talisman, or maybe a light, guiding, promising, and showing a path. At times when questions about rights, or citizenship for women, or Black people are far from settled, some call on her to preside like something akin to a saint, with arms raised and rosary dangling from outstretched fingers, there for all who seek her protection from the rising tide of American fascism.

3

MEETING BETHUNE

My visit to Daytona Beach took place in the midst of the COVID pandemic. In November 2021, my husband, Bill, and I, armed with disinfecting wipes and lots of masks, boarded a plane for the first time in over a year. We were headed to see the newly unveiled statue of Bethune that was due to travel up the East Coast from Florida, with a stop in South Carolina, before arriving at its new home in Washington, DC, in the Capitol Building's Statuary Hall. What drew us out was my unshakable need to see Mary McLeod Bethune's chiseled commemoration in her hometown. I wanted to see it feted and celebrated by those who had strategized for years to make sure she would be the Floridian chosen to represent the state in Statuary Hall. I wanted to get a sense of who would show up to see her and how they would feel when they saw the finished version. I had heard that it was magnificent, in a highly detailed, impressive, even haunting sort of way. I thought to learn something about what the residents of the town thought about the long and expensive process that led to their organizing across lines of race, geography, and class to honor their hometown daughter. I wondered what, if anything, those who might be in the viewing hall with me thought about her, a Black woman born of parents who were enslaved, displacing the Confederate general Edmund Kirby Smith as one of the two statues to represent Florida to the nation.

I had prepared for the trip as scholars do when we leave home to research something. I knew which archives in the area were open and how long a quick stop in them would take if I wanted to meet librarians and archivists. I knew where Bethune's house was, as well as her grave, and had planned a day for Bill—who good-naturedly offered to drive us around during the three-day sojourn—and me to visit her statue, see the library at Bethune-Cookman, tour her former home, and pay our respects at her final resting place before heading off for dinner and a chat about what we had seen. Armed with my iPhone, Google Maps, and weeks' worth of research notes, we pulled into the parking lot of the exhibition center where Bethune's statue was open to the public. This trip was about breadth, not depth, and though I knew I wanted to see the statue, I was thinking of it as a sort of stop just to check this one thing off my list before moving on to the next thing. That is why I can't fully explain what happened when I turned the corner and moved closer to the eleven-foot mountain of marble. I found her eyes with mine; it was as if there were a blood-pumping heart. When I realized there were tears rolling down my cheeks, I felt a swell of emotion that may have been appreciation or simply an understanding of what it meant for this statue to exist, for Bethune to have lived, for this particular honor to be bestowed. The statue is chiseled from marble mined from the same quarry, the same vein of marble, that Michelangelo used to make his statue of David in the early 1500s. It is still stunning in 2023. This is the last piece of the vein of pure white statuary marble from that quarry, and it is so precious and difficult to attain that other artists offered to pay two or three times the cost to acquire the 11.5-ton block before the master sculpture Nilda Comas could even begin sculpting it. The resulting statue tips the scales at 6,129 pounds—3 tons. Michelangelo's David was the Alpha form shaped from that specific marble, and Comas's Bethune is the Omega.

I know it all sounds a bit like a scene from a not very good movie, the kind where the soundtrack begins to swell to prompt listeners that something important is happening, that emotions are being called forth. The longer I looked into those eyes, the closer I came to losing restraint. As it was, the act of holding back the "ugly crying" was turning into enough of a challenge that I started both holding my breath and calculating the distance to the nearest door, just in case I had to make a fast exit lest I embarrass myself. I stayed indoors, but with my stomach and throat fluttering with the effort of containing unstable emotion. Calm returned as I stopped looking at her eyes and focused hard on her chic ankle boots with their little sculpted pearl buttons, the smooth curve at the bend of the stone walking cane she held, and the way the sculptor chiseled marble in a way that made it seem to drape and lie as if made of fabric, not stone. I also took in the black rose clutched in her stone hand. It had been sculpted from black marble from Spain. In 1927, Bethune visited a garden in Europe filled with roses displaying a rainbow of colors. She saw it as an interracial garden and had a vision of how all people could peacefully thrive together, side by side. Sometimes she would speak about a "people garden" and explain that the people of the world were like flowers growing in a garden. Red, yellow, small, or tall, all were different, but each was lovely. Once, a child who heard her describe this world said Black people couldn't live in a people garden, because there weren't any black flowers. Bethune replied, "Just because you have not seen a thing doesn't mean it doesn't exist." People started to call Bethune the Black Rose, and she started referring to her students as black roses. She had seventy-two black rosebushes shipped from Switzerland to Bethune-Cookman to drive home the point.[1]

Looking at her statue as a collection of its elements was enough of a distraction to allow me to calm, contain, and steady myself. I was not the only person that day who strolled, viewed, wiped tears, and glanced around to see if anyone was looking. None of us wanted communal wailing, but when we saw the shimmer in the eyes of our fellow onlookers, we smiled sheepishly and looked hurriedly away. A *Daytona Beach News-Journal* article from a few months before described something similar happening when a group from the Daytona area traveled to the Tuscan coast of Italy to view the nearly finished version of the sculpture. Hiram Powell, then the president of Bethune-Cookman, told the reporter that he expected to be dazzled by the artfully chiseled statue, but what shocked him was the "soul-shaking moment" when the cloth draped over the gleaming white work of art was pulled away and he found himself sliding and kneeling on one knee. He said, "Her eyes met mine, and something just came over me, I can't describe it. She is such a figure and influence on my life. It was meeting the eyes of the maker of all that."[2]

In the summer of 2022, the marble statue of Bethune replaced the one of Confederate general Edmund Kirby

A PASSIONATE MIND IN RELENTLESS PURSUIT

Smith, whose bronzed likeness had represented the state since 1922. Sources about Smith's life point out that though he was born in Saint Augustine, Florida, his family moved to Tennessee when he was a young child. He was chosen to represent the state of Florida less because of his place of birth than because of his role fighting for the Confederacy, the states that chose to secede from the United States and take up arms against what had been their government, plunging the nation into the Civil War. During the war, Smith rose to the rank of general, one of only seven in the Confederate Army, and near the end of the war, he commanded what was called the Trans-Mississippi Department, comprised of Arkansas, Missouri, Texas, western Louisiana, Arizona Territory, and a broad swath of land known simply as "Indian Territory." The nation he fought to build as a general in the Army of the Confederate States of America was a republic based on the ideology of white supremacy. Convinced that white supremacy and slavery were threatened by Abraham Lincoln's 1860 election to the presidency on a platform opposing the expansion of slavery into the western territories of the developing nation, the Confederacy, which derived its wealth and influence from slavery, declared its secession from the United States. Most of the states where slavery was legal banded together to form their own country where they could continue to enslave human beings. These states included South Carolina, Mississippi, Florida, Alabama, Georgia, Louisiana, Texas, Virginia, Arkansas, Tennessee, North Carolina, Kentucky, and Missouri, and they set up their own government complete with money, a president, a vice president, and a Confederate Congress. In his Cornerstone Speech, the Confederate vice president, Alexander Stephens, described the ideology of the Confederate States of America as centrally based "upon the great truth that the negro is not equal to the white man; that slavery and subordination to the superior race, is his natural and normal condition."[3]

After the fall of Vicksburg in 1863 severed the Confederacy in two, Smith found himself cut off from communication with the Confederate capital of Richmond, Virginia, and so declared himself in charge of all aspects of all troops and military strategy in the entire Trans-Mississippi area. He summarily awarded himself virtually unlimited administrative, military, and political authority. His power absolute, the area under his command became known as "Kirby Smithdom." Smith negotiated and signed terms of surrender in Galveston, Texas, in June of 1865, nearly two months after Robert E. Lee surrendered to the Union Army at Appomattox, and he immediately left the country for Mexico and then to Cuba to escape prosecution for treason. Remaining committed to the ideology of white supremacy, he joined the Ku Klux Klan in Florida immediately following his return from Cuba to the United States.[4]

All the past and current Confederate statues displayed in Statuary Hall and elsewhere on Capitol Hill represented men with ideologies like Smith's; they were all placed on federal ground in either the 1920s or 1950s as part of a concerted effort to offer an idealized view of the Confederacy and the successionist South. In this revisioning, the South fought for a "just cause," which had to do with protecting their way of life and had nothing to do with white people protecting the society they had built on the ideology of white supremacy. Funded and spearheaded by organizations such as the United Daughters of the Confederacy and the Sons of Confederate Veterans, the heaviest periods of lobbying for this particular view of the South's role in the Civil War was during periods of intense organizing by movements in support of racial equality. In an August 2017 article for National Public Radio, journalist Miles Parks quotes historian Jane Dailey from the University of Chicago as saying, "The purpose of the monuments was not to celebrate the past but rather to promote a white supremacist future." According to a December 2018 article from *Smithsonian Magazine* on the amounts of money federal and local governments spend on such monuments, "Far from simply being markers of historic events and people, as proponents argue," statues and memorials such as the bronze statue of Smith that stood in Statuary Hall of the US Capitol for close to one hundred years, "were created and funded by Jim Crow governments to pay homage to a slave-owning society and to serve as blunt assertions of dominance over Black people." It was rarely the case that Black citizens had a say about which figures or ideologies should represent the states they lived in. These were erected and installed without the consent or even input of Black people, who remembered the Civil War far differently, and who had no interest in honoring those who fought to keep them enslaved and then later fought as hard to deny them their rights.[5]

Perhaps nothing best encapsulates this point about racism and the power of commemoration than understanding how close we as a nation came to memorializing the fictional figure of the Black mammy. This was also in the 1920s, another attempt to keep alive the myth of the beneficent slaveholding South. As Congressman Charles Stedman of North Carolina said in support of a Senate bill to honor the "faithful colored mammies" of the South, "The traveler, as he passes by, will recall that epoch of southern civilization" when "fidelity and loyalty" prevailed. He added, "No class of any race of people held in bondage could be found anywhere who lived more free from care or distress." A majority of senators agreed that Representative Stedman had a good point and passed the bill approving a new monument, along with a grant of land on which a statue would be built to pay homage to the "memory of the faithful slave mammies of the South." Though Stedman moved the bill from conception to a vote in the Senate, the idea was originally hatched by a group of white women, members of the United Daughters of the Confederacy, who brought pressure to bear on southern elected officials to support their cause and rally to their aid. While their persuasion worked in the Senate, the bill stalled in the House of Representatives after fierce opposition from Black women, including Mary Church Terrell and other members of the National Association of Colored Women's Clubs, the year before Bethune was elected president of the organization. That resistance ended up being key in stopping the process, which had gotten so far along that a model was constructed, molded by a Black artist named Ulric Stonewall Jackson Dunbar. No monument was actually ever built, as three months after the introduction of the bill in the Senate, Congress adjourned without taking any further action. The spot where Mammy was to have stood is now occupied by a statue of Tomas Garrigue Masaryk, the first president of Czechoslovakia.[6]

While both General Smith and Mrs. Bethune were citizens of Florida at some point in their lives, they represented very different things about the reality of citizenship in that state. Surely there is some meaning to be made of the fact that the citizens of the state of Florida selected Bethune to represent them, and that she became the first Black woman so honored in Statuary Hall. Going forward, instead of a Confederate general who vigorously defended white supremacy, Florida would be represented by a Black woman who was the first in her family to be born free and spent her life strategizing to overthrow racism and white supremacy. I choose to view her as a repudiation of all he had stood for. The whole episode is a reminder about how frequently this nation, founded on documents professing individual freedoms, keeps finding itself called upon to account for its deep entanglements with genocide, slavery, brutality, and theft.

Just as the installation of a statue paying homage to a Confederate general like Smith revealed specific racial dynamics about power and who wielded it in Florida in the 1920s, Bethune's statue spoke to a considerably different dynamic. It came to the nation's capital following a yearslong process and included the opportunity for citizens of the state to lobby, listen, decide, and vote. Though he is a sitting senator from the state of Florida today, in March 2018 Rick Scott was the Florida governor who signed legislation that capped the two-year process seeking public input from citizens about who should represent them in Statuary Hall.

Those who wished to participate had five opportunities to do so, including through an online survey, emails, and letters. In whatever medium, citizens who engaged in the process were asked to name a nominee and to include a bit about the person's area of influence, their significant contribution to the state, whether the nominator was an individual or a member of an organization, and their county of residence. The debate and process were both robust and extensive. Initially, when the Great Floridians Ad Hoc Committee of Florida's Division of Historical Resources met in June 2016, there were almost 300 names under consideration, though the committee had determined that only 130 of them met the eligibility criteria. Bethune received nominations from 1,237 of the 3,200 people offering public comment, so it seems likely that she was a leading contender from the outset. That 2016 meeting was just the first stage of the process and resulted in the committee choosing three names to submit to the Florida legislature for consideration. They voted 321–1 to have Bethune represent the best of who they were. This was actually the second process that culminated in Bethune's image on a statue in Washington, DC. The first federal memorial to her was dedicated in 1974 and is actually larger than the 2022 statue: Bethune stands twelve feet high and is shown passing her "legacy" to nine-foot-tall boy and girl statues.[7]

The story of this first statue begins in 1959 with an idea hatched by Dorothy Height, then president of the National Council of Negro Women, who believed erecting a statue of Bethune in the nation's capital was a fitting way to mark the 1963 centennial celebration of the signing of the Emancipation Proclamation. She and others also thought it time to replace the then almost one-hundred-year-old statue featuring President Lincoln holding the Emancipation Proclamation before a kneeling Black man, modeled after Archer Alexander, the last person captured under the Fugitive Slave Act, whose arms are extended upward to show that his shackles have been broken. The monument's dedication had taken place in the park on April 14, 1876, the eleventh anniversary of President Lincoln's death, and the money for the "kneeling slave" statue was overwhelmingly raised, penny by hard-won penny, by emancipated Black people living in DC.[8]

On the day the Lincoln statue was unveiled, twenty-five thousand people showed up and crowded around to listen to orator, abolitionist, writer, and strategist Frederick Douglass deliver the keynote address at the ceremony. Members of the audience included President Ulysses S. Grant, his cabinet, and members of Congress. Douglass did not come that day to praise Lincoln or to thank the federal government. He talked instead about how the monument perpetuated many stereotypes about Black people, not the least of which was in denying the ways enslaved Black people actively partici-pated in freeing themselves. He didn't agree, and history did not support the view, that most of the enslaved had waited passively for Lincoln to free them, as the statue seemed to suggest. In addition, Douglass pointed out Lincoln's char-acter and legacy, saying, "Truth compels me to admit, even here in the presence of the monument we have erected to his memory, Abraham Lincoln was not, in the fullest sense of the word, either our man or our model. In his interests, in his associations, in his habits of thought, and in his prejudices, he was a white man." Not content to let that one assertion be the end of his analysis of Lincoln, Douglass said that Lincoln was "preeminently the white man's president, entirely de-voted to the welfare of white men," and concluded, "He was ready and willing at any time during the first years of his administration to deny, postpone, and sacrifice the rights of humanity in the colored people to promote the welfare of the white people of this country."[9]

These are the issues Bethune's first statue in DC was called upon to engage and correct. Featuring Bethune hand-ing a copy of her legacy to two young Black children, it is a very different view of legacy, gratitude, and joy in Black free-dom from the one featuring the kneeling slave. In a final act of symbolism, once the statue of Bethune was installed in Lincoln Park, the "kneeling slave" statue was twisted and turned so that instead of facing Capitol Hill, it faced Bethune. Alexandria Russell has pointed out in her unpublished dissertation on Black women and public memorialization that organizations embracing memorialization as a political strategy were skilled at raising money to support the memorials they conceptualized. "Their leadership provided the foundation for the emergence of traditional public history mediums centered on the distinct history of Black women that imagined a Black woman as a central connection between the past, present, and future histories of Black people in America." The late Dorothy Height put it another way, explaining that it is best to understand that memorials are not simply statues but "tangible evidence that black people have achieved greatness and that our government recognizes this truth—the black child needs this as well as the necessities of life." Speaking specifically about Bethune and the 1974 likeness of her installed in Emancipation Park, Russell notes that the statue represented a "national shift" in memorializing Black women who, while generally underrepresented in national commemorations depicting women or Black people, had their activism legitimized through the federal government "as figures of national importance and noteworthy contributors to America." Bethune came to symbolize character, activism, service, and history. Her commemoration led to an outpouring of similarly inspired memorialization in local communities that "created memorial parks, house museums, and historical markers highlighting Black women across the nation."[10]

Led by Height, the NCNW had launched an effort to swap out the passive cultural associations between emancipation, kneeling, and a benevolent Lincoln and instead link freedom to education, progress, and Black political participation by commemorating the Emancipation Proclamation through Bethune's memorialization. Things got off to a promising start. Congressional approval came quickly, as did support from President Dwight Eisenhower, who in 1960 approved of the idea to erect a memorial statue of Bethune in DC's Lincoln Park. The NCNW, by then feeling that the way was clear, selected one of the nation's most celebrated sculpture artists, Robert Berks, to imagine the memorial, and they began a multifaceted campaign to raise the money they would need to see the project through. Soon, however, the organization found that raising money for a statue in that era—while the war in Vietnam raged, Black poverty spiraled, Senator Daniel Patrick Moynihan issued a report proclaiming Black families pathological and Black women emasculating, and the civil rights movement transitioned to the Black power movement—was perhaps a case of misguided priorities. Few were outright opposed to the

Bethune memorial, but more and more frequently, staff at the NCNW headquarters began to report to the leadership that they were getting letters from across the country expressing concern about priorities. One such letter to Congresswoman Shirley Chisholm, the honorary chair of the Bethune Memorial Fund Committee, said it was a "gross hypocrisy" for the Nixon administration and Congress to authorize building the memorial, which would be taken care of by the National Park Service, but "refuse to help with the costs" associated with having it built, especially "at this time, when so many black children are undernourished and starving and black youths in ghettos are desperately in need of better education, jobs, and hope." Other women who wrote to Height agreed that a more tangible use of money in "a living monument dedicated to the teachings and ideals of Mary Bethune would be far more fitting." Raising and spending money was a consistent topic of concern, and most of the letter writers said they would prefer it if the NCNW would think about raising money to "help feed people in Mississippi," establishing "cooperative farms," or "building a hospital." Another person wrote that, while they understood the memorial would be "no doubt a beautiful statue," they asked, "What good will that do for the folks who need bread, medical assistance, learning, etc.?" A few felt that the organizers were actually misappropriating Bethune's legacy because "anybody who knows who she was, and what she did for sufferers, knows that she is a memorial in herself."[11]

Though the NCNW did change strategy somewhat to prioritize support for local activists in various communities across the nation, and to provide much-needed aid to civil rights projects, they still raised money for the monument. By 1971 they had enough to break ground in Lincoln Park. Some NCNW members traveled to Washington, DC, for the groundbreaking ceremony, and other chapters recognized the moment through local celebrations in their cities. Houston mayor Louie Welch issued a proclamation to declare May 30, 1971, Dr. Mary McLeod Bethune Memorial Fund Day and "urge[d] all citizens to join . . . in supporting the Houston Section of the National Council of Negro Women, Inc., in its efforts to raise $2,000 toward the cost of building the memorial monument to Dr. Bethune." Scholar Jenny Woodley also explores the extent to which organizations outside the NCNW banded together to raise money for the Bethune memorial, noting that "the Howard D. Woodson High School Choir of Washington, D.C., decided to embark on a concert tour through D.C., Virginia, North Carolina and South Carolina to raise funds for the memorial," and the Pan African Center for Empowerment in Seattle, Washington, asked to collaborate with the Seattle chapter of the

NCNW to prominently display a replica of the Bethune statue to showcase the contributions of Black people to the nation.[12]

These efforts paid off. On what would have been Bethune's ninety-ninth birthday, July 10, 1974, one month before President Nixon resigned, one step ahead of impeachment for his role in the Watergate debacle, the Mary McLeod Bethune Memorial in Lincoln Park, Washington, DC, was finally unveiled. *Jet* magazine covered the occasion and gave a strong sense of the day's importance, describing the feeling as the assembled dignitaries collectively tugged on the rope, and the light blue fabric fell from the twelve-foot, four-thousand-pound memorial, and applause thundered and cheers rang out. Then the singing began, with the Bethune-Cookman College choir leading the crowd of eighteen thousand in a rendition of "Lift Every Voice and Sing," written by Floridian brothers James Weldon and J. Rosamond Johnson, known as the Negro National Anthem.[13]

There were, of course, lots of thanks to go around, beginning with Robert Berks, the artist who sculpted the memorial. Then Walter Washington, the first Black mayor of DC, proclaimed July 10 Mary McLeod Bethune Day. Congresswoman Shirley Chisholm, the first Black woman elected to Congress, who had run for president a few years before, commended Dorothy Height, president of the NCNW, for her leadership and vision while stewarding the process that had brought them there that day, and for her abiding faith and patience.[14] Secretary of the Interior Rogers C. B. Morton expressed his personal "gratitude" to the NCNW for the organization's "contribution to the National Park system" and delivered an official message on behalf of President Richard Nixon, who sent word to the assembled group that "it is highly appropriate . . . that we memorialize the life and achievements of Mary McLeod Bethune."[15] Following these remarks, actor Cicely Tyson explained that although Bethune had little to leave in "worldly possessions," her desire was to leave "distilled principles and policies" that were representative of the essence of her "life's work." She then launched into a dramatic reading of Bethune's Last Will and Testament, which had been published after her death in 1955 in *Ebony* magazine. The engraved plaque mounted on the front of the memorial includes portions of this will and testament, including the phrases "I Leave You Love," "I Leave You Hope," "I Leave You Faith," and "I Leave You Finally a Responsibility to Our Young People." Another actor, Roscoe Lee Browne, read from Frederick Douglass's 1876 address at the unveiling of the "kneeling slave" statue. Browne replaced Abraham Lincoln's name with Bethune's in Douglass's speech, declaring, "On this day in this place in this speech, man becomes woman." After reveling in the festivities, thousands walked from Lincoln Park to the steps of the

Capitol in the People's Parade of Dedication, organized in collaboration with Martin Luther King, Jr., and Coretta Scott King's mentor, Bayard Rustin.[16] This "Celebration March" involved Black organizations from all over the nation, called together "to inspire rededication to the legacy of Mary Bethune and the highest principles of a democratic society." The commemorative events, concerts, symposia, and cultural festivals and performances continued all over the city.[17]

The so-called "kneeling slave" statue with which Bethune's memorial is in dialogue remains in Lincoln Park. The same cannot be said of the statue of Smith, the Confederate general she displaced in Statuary Hall in 2022. As of the summer of that year, it was still not clear where the statue of Kirby Smith would be displayed or housed: Florida officials were having difficulty finding anyone who wanted to take him in. Commissioners in Tavares, Lake County's county seat, reversed the support they had given to the Lake County Historical Society and Museum to house the Smith statue in the historic courthouse. As justification for the change, they said the arrival of the Confederate general's statue in Lake County would mean placing it in the same courthouse where, in the 1950s, the innocent Black men who came to be known as the Groveland Four had been wrongly convicted. It would send the wrong message for our contemporary era.

The Groveland Four were Black men we now know were wrongly accused of raping a white woman in 1949. Two of them were killed, and the other two were convicted and imprisoned on false evidence. Though in her seventies at the time, Bethune worked furiously to raise funds for their defense and loudly decried their convictions and murders. The officials said, "The Lake County Historic Courthouse has a difficult history of its own and the use of our historic building as the permanent home for the Smith statue has created division in our community for the last few years." As I write this, it is unclear where one might go to see Smith's statue. If you would like to see Bethune, she is in Statuary Hall of the Capitol Building in Washington, DC, and in Lincoln Park, which is just a little more than a mile away.[18]

4

"YOURS FOR NEGRO
WOMANHOOD"

Mary McLeod Bethune had dreamed of starting a school for Black girls since she had first attended one herself as a twelve-year-old. When in 1904 she learned from one of her contacts in the Methodist Church that formal education for Black children was virtually nonexistent in Daytona, Florida, and that the community might be interested in starting one, she packed up her things and her family and set out, determined to succeed. She had no trouble finding the Black neighborhood and community once she arrived. It was the area of town with no streetlights, sidewalks, or functional sewage system. Luck found her soon after she arrived in town with little more than $1.50 to her name. She met a white woman in the grocery store, and, as had become her way after having graduated from the Moody Bible Institute, where she had learned to preach and spread the gospel, Bethune painted a word picture that bubbled over with enough passion to inspire her conversation partner, an influential white clubwoman named Dora Maley. Up until that point, Maley had not given much thought to the education of Black children. A member of the Palmetto Women's Club, by the time she parted ways with Bethune that day, she had emptied "out the contents of [her] change purse" and immediately called a meeting of her fellow club members to talk about ways they could support the school and Bethune. She also, in short order, convinced her brother-in-law to give Bethune "free use" of a cabin he owned in the Black section of town.[1]

Despite Maley's support and that of other powerful white residents kindly disposed toward Black children having a school to attend, times were hard, and it was unclear if the school would survive. The roof leaked, the wood in the home was rotted through, and both Bethune and her pupils were often hungry. In her unpublished memoir, she recalled, "We burned logs and used charred splinters as pencils, and mashed elderberries for ink. I begged strangers for a broom, a lamp, a bit of cretonne to put around the packing case which served as my desk. I haunted the city dump and trash piles behind hotels, retrieving discarded linen and kitchenware, cracked dishes, broken chairs, pieces of old lumber. Everything was scoured and mended." She was twenty-nine when the school opened with a first class of six students—five girls aged six through twelve and Bethune's five-year-old son, Albertus—on October 4, 1904.

Bethune welcomed each child every morning with a sing-song greeting: "Come in little girl, we've been expecting you. I hope you'll be happy with us." She named the school the Daytona Literary and Industrial Institute, but it didn't take long for members of Daytona's Black community to start calling it "the Bethune School." She charged a weekly tuition of fifty cents for those who could pay in money. For those who could not, she accepted chickens, eggs, and produce as payment. Bethune initially was responsible for every aspect of the school's operation, teaching all the students and subjects in all the grade levels. She was also spending considerable time and effort raising the money to keep the school afloat. Quickly realizing that tuition would never be enough to cover the cost of the school, she was determined to hire teachers who could help keep the school open and functioning while giving her the urgently needed time to inspire those with means to donate to the school. In recounting the period, she said, "I need strong women to help me realize this vision." She also needed to have the school accredited so it would be eligible to receive state funds. The first hire Bethune made was Frances Reynolds Keyser, a graduate of Hunter

College who had been the supervisor of the White Rose Mission for delinquent girls in New York City. Keyser arrived five years after Bethune's school first opened, in 1909, and took over its entire educational program. She was a literary critic of note, able to boast that the famed poet Paul Laurence Dunbar submitted his poems to her for feedback before sending them out for publication. In a few short years, Keyser's educational programs earned the school state accreditation, easing its financial burdens, if only slightly. Bethune also hired Portia Smiley, a graduate of Hampton Normal and Agricultural Institute and the Pratt Institute, to supervise the domestic science program. Bethune described Smiley, who had practical nursing skills, as "an artist" in the realm of domestic science.[2]

Together, these women joined Bethune as she began to craft and polish the strategies melding education and political organizing that would define her life from that point on. Her founding that school became an argument about how education, classrooms, and schoolhouses were much more than places to learn the basics of reading, math, and science. They were community institutions, building blocks of empowerment and political organizing. The farms where students were taught to grow and harvest food for the students and faculty became an important source of nourishment for the whole community. The school offered reading courses for adults needing to pass literacy tests so they could vote in county elections. The students organized fundraisers and bake sales to raise the necessary money to pay the poll taxes for community members who wanted to vote but couldn't afford the fee. When students at the school were unable to receive adequate health care, Bethune founded a hospital and a nurse training program to see to the health of students and the broader community as well.

Bethune's school and philosophy of education combined teaching, education, entrepreneurship, mutual aid, and electoral politics. It was a vision of how best to push back against white supremacy and its declaration of Black inferiority. She trained Black women freedom fighters who read, organized, voted to empower Black people as they stood tall and strong in the warmth of their communal sun. It started with education but didn't end there. Her goal from that point on, she once wrote, was for others to be able to say, if "Mrs. Bethune can but get into the doorway, she will stand there and hold the door open so that other women may pass through." When she founded her school, we know now that she was writing the opening chapter of a book about her strategy to make Black freedom possible. Bethune did not believe Black women and girls would survive life in the United States if they remained relegated to a lesser place in politics and culture, treated as shivering figures outside the house, peeking in a window as the chosen enjoyed the warmth of citizenship and acceptance.[3]

As I researched Bethune, I remembered the first time I understood the power of a vision centering women, felt the courage to imagine a world from the perspective of women and girls. I was twelve and read Toni Morrison's book *The Bluest Eye* and for the first time fully inhabited a fictional world made for Black girls. The emotional landscape spoke to me, and I knew the difference between joining fictional characters in their universe and a novel lighting a path for me to find a way through my own. When I read *The Bluest Eye,* I had recently begun to attend an integrated school and was often the only Black girl in any of my classrooms. In those classrooms, there were no others like me to whom I could turn to compare notes on decoding the language between adult eyes looking at me and their gaze when looking at their "own" children whose skin shared their tint. In my singularity, I couldn't describe it, but I knew something important took place between that and what happened when they flicked their notice in my direction. It wasn't just their eyes. I was also familiar with the too-large and too-long-held grin that meant something, but I wasn't quite sure what. *The*

Bluest Eye helped me to understand the distinction worth knowing, that there is a difference between acceptance and toleration. I turned the last page, understanding.[4]

The Bluest Eye is about Black girls and the women they grow into. It describes intimacies that build bonds and the disillusionments that strain them, sometimes beyond breaking. It plumbs the depths of the matter of why some Black women fail to survive the fallout when their families and communities are battered by the violence of white supremacy. It is a primer for how communities of Black women and girls are taught to develop their own stroke to power toward safety in the seas of economic violence and exploitative employment arrangements. It was the first book that helped me to understand the mundane and immediate nature of evil, and how beauty and ugliness are weapons forged in the same kiln. It makes visible the fragile yet precious bonds between Black girls and women when they delight, and even when they disdain. It offers truths about the nature of Black love and its ability to both protect and destroy. It is about a Black girl driven mad by the wafting of the hydra-headed tentacles of white disgust with Black skin and the people who possessed it, and explains how contempt is weaponized and hurt curdles as it curls itself around and within Black homes, psyches, and communities. Toni Morrison's first novel explains about faces and forces that could shape and malform. It was those same faces and forces that made the world Bethune survived, and the one she visioned and with dogged strength attempted to build with and for Black women. A woman who sometimes signed formal letters "Yours for Negro Woman-hood," she and Morrison shared fundamental beliefs.[5]

In 1909, Bethune attended her first meeting of the National Association of Colored Women's Clubs (NACWC). The passionate speech she gave about her school inspired the attendees to take up a collection and led NACWC's founding president, Mary Church Terrell, to predict Bethune would one day become president of the organization. A decade and a half later, in 1924, the membership elected Bethune to represent them as their national president. At that first gathering, Bethune met luminaries and received financial support for her school, and she had the opportunity to inspire, be inspired by, and strategize the future of freedom with women like Terrell, the Oberlin-educated voting rights activist whom she had long admired. She met and learned from Ida B. Wells-Barnett, the courageous, crusading journalist and activist, and one of the founding members of the National Association for the Advancement of Colored People (NAACP). The presentations at that year's conference explored what the Black women in attendance could collectively do to address a wide range of discrimination they and their communities regularly encountered. Lectures touched on topics ranging from the prevalence of racial violence and harassment to panels decrying the lack of reliable employment opportunities for all Black people, and especially Black women who found themselves locked in jobs as domestics or agricultural workers with few educational or societal prospects that would make other jobs a consistent possibility. In addition, though the Nineteenth Amendment guaranteeing women the right to vote would not be ratified and passed for another seven years, women's suffrage, equality, and citizenship consumed a considerable amount of attention. At the time, only nine states allowed women to vote.

Bethune did not leave much to help us understand her experiences and feelings about attending the conference, but it is safe to assume it would have been a productive and heady time, as she joined in community with other Black women organizing against oppression and violence. In addition to their politics, she was intrigued by the demeanor, decorum, and style of the Black women who led the organization. As one of her biographers, Rackham Holt, put it, "Up to then, Mrs. Bethune had been well enough satisfied with her appearance, content to be neat and clean and clothed in sober decorum, as befitted a missionary. But in this company her feminine vanity began to assert itself. She began to be clothes conscious." We know Bethune embraced her fellow attendees' fashion sense right along with their activism and analysis of politics. Fashion is, and always has been, politics. What that means is that the leadership of the NACWC represented a social and political class of Black women in the early years of the twentieth century who talked about clothes and style as an important strategy for combating cultural assumptions about Black women and their being unfit for leadership or politics. In the glare of a full-length cultural mirror held firmly in place by the glue of anti-Blackness, the curl of the hair, cut of a frock, fit of a glove represented a political strategy and a signal that they were worthy of inclusion in the highest echelons of Black society and of serious consideration by white people.[6]

This stitching together of fashion with politics was not about how well accepted one might be if they chose to pair, for example, a brown shoe with a black dress, or idle wondering about which accessories might be productively left home on that day. At that time, and for these women, fashion and dress were weapons in the war to achieve citizenship. Many of the women who were part of the NACWC took self-presentation as a political strategy. They imagined part of the secret for defeating racism lay in the bodies of the Black people who knew how to dress, act, and be in public. If they mastered the codes, those who embraced such thinking said, cultural and social doors would open for them, their families, and even perhaps whole communities of Black people. Notes of that narrative play a recognizable tune in an article written in a Black women's magazine called *Ringwood's Journal of African American Fashion* by Mary Church Terrell. She wanted readers of the magazine to understand that "every woman, no matter what her circumstances, owes it to herself, her family and her friends to look as well as her means will permit."

This is how it came to be that during this period, some women believed the gentle rustle of a skirt swishing around a neatly hidden ankle could refute cultural charges and beliefs about Black women's sexual availability, or that the breath-throttling clinch of a tightly laced corset could be the first step to freeing Black women from economic violence. During the early decades of the twentieth century, members of the NACWC, like those Bethune first met in 1909, discussed dress, fashion, and style as markers of class status for all women, but particularly for those who were Black and from struggling personal backgrounds, such as Bethune. According to scholars who have written about her during this period, though Bethune outwardly may have seemed to cross class lines, given that she dressed, spoke, and moved with the confidence of one who belonged, her "family background, financial position, and dark skin color prevented her complete acceptance by these women and her entry into the ranks of their class." For her part, whether she felt accepted or not, more than a decade later, Bethune would assume the presidency of the NACWC and try and fail to get the membership to agree to her view of how politics could and should work. She believed "a woman is free if she lives by her own standards and creates her own destiny, if she prizes her individuality and puts no boundaries on her hopes for tomorrow." She sought to encourage women to dress as they wished, but to disconnect the hard-and-fast beliefs about clothes and status.[7]

As Bethune assumed the reins of the NACWC, her contemporaries took note that as her path came to consistently cross those of the higher-status members of the organization, she embraced the idea of fashion as self-creation. A few of her acquaintances even mentioned disapprovingly that she collected and wore eyeglasses with nonprescription lenses decades before her eyes and health required it. She simply liked the way she looked in them. In addition to eyeglass frames, she favored a stylish shoe and had favorite strands of pearls she liked to don when sitting for a formal portrait or giving a particular speech. She started to wear more hats in public, tilting them on her head just so. Also, though she did not need any help with her mobility, she accessorized her outfits with a growing collection of walking canes, such as the one she showed off in a May 1953 photograph in *Jet* magazine that captured her displaying the late President FDR's cane, gifted to her by longtime friend Eleanor Roosevelt. On that occasion, she was overheard saying, "Just as some women smoke cigarettes, I swagger canes."[8]

As Bethune's status rose over the two decades between founding her school in 1904 and her election as the president of the NACWC in 1924, her perspective broadened to envision a world where Black women's issues and needs were not confined to specific regions or countries but had national and international resonance. This issue was at the heart of her campaign to become the eighth president of NACWC, a campaign that pitted her against Ida B. Wells-Barnett, who had long wanted to helm the organization and campaigned hard for the office. The membership cast their vote for Bethune because they thought she was less confrontational and more pleasant than Wells-Barnett, but they soon discovered that despite her seemingly low-key demeanor, Bethune's vision was a radical one. It represented a complete break from the views of past leaders and proved challenging to many of the group's members, who were more comfortable keeping things as they were. No more, if Bethune had her way, would the NACWC spend so much time and energy castigating lower-income Black people for their poor style choices, their hairstyles, or their thick accents that didn't as easily blend in with the ways northern high-status Black people communicated. Now they would turn their attention to the larger structural issues that Bethune believed were more important obstacles to opportunity and progress.

Though her ideas sounded good enough, as they say, "on paper," it was another thing entirely for her to remake the organization from one that primarily focused on providing individual Black people with opportunities for self-help via education and vocational training into a powerful lobbying group that would grow beyond the United States and advocate for policies that systemically transformed the economic and political basis of Black women in the United States and around the world. Initially, NACWC members expressed great enthusiasm for Bethune's ideas, but the changes necessary to put them into practice soon began to rankle. Two years into her term, in August 1926, Bethune wrote that the biggest problem facing the association was finding the "connecting threads" that unite women nationwide. In June 1928, she pleaded with the membership to "forget everything that looks like individualism" and begin to build a sturdy structure that will "hold Black women everywhere."[9]

It did not take long for this new focus to cause tension between Bethune and Terrell, who had remained active in the organization and was then serving as the national legislative chairman of the group. Bethune and Terrell were barely a decade apart in age, but they came of political age in different eras and embraced differing theories of change. Terrell had molded the association into a vehicle for self-help whose objective was to improve the moral and cultural standards of her "less favored and more ignorant sisters." Under Terrell's leadership, the NACWC sought to show the "masses" of Black women the behaviors and attitudes in need of embracing if they wished to enhance their lives; it was "a vehicle for the emergence of middle-class women." Terrell clung fast to these goals and told Bethune she thought the organization should remain decentralized, allowing for local, state, and national chapters to define which types of self-help projects they wanted to embrace. She did not believe that the national office should dictate particular strategies.[10]

For her part, Bethune believed the organization should go beyond individual-focused projects organized along the general lines of "self-help" and take a page from the political work that organizations like A. Philip Randolph's Brotherhood of Sleeping Car Porters were doing to join national efforts to organize the working class. She wanted to advocate for structural change and push the NACWC to move away from primarily focusing on charity and social service work, and to move much more firmly toward fighting for social justice. She urged the women of the NACWC to develop a unified political voice at the national level, saying she wanted Black women to realize that they should no longer confine their duties to the home but instead "must have some voice in the laws which shall govern her and her children and send her sons to death."

During her administration, the NACWC began to act like lobbyists or representatives from foreign nations, sending "delegates" from the organization to congressional hearings as members began lobbying elected officials on behalf of the group. Bethune believed progress would best be achieved by moving away from gradualism and began to advocate for systemic change to improve the lives of Black people who were living without civil protections and at the mercy of whites in positions of authority. Because the NACWC was an organization representing the interests of Black women, Bethune believed it had a responsibility to "assume an attitude toward all big questions involving the welfare of the nation, public right and especially the present and future of our race" and that questions facing the women of the NACWC were both national and international, and included humanitarian, moral, social, and economic problems. Bethune said, "This brings forward the 'color question' belting the world, colonial dominions, and their attendant evils; political freedom and territorial problems of governments." As was true of other leaders, like Paul Robeson, Bayard Rustin, A. Philip

Randolph, and W. E. B. Du Bois, Bethune insisted on seeing the whole field as she strove to push American democracy to live up to its principles, not only in theory but in practice.[11]

Terrell disagreed. She considered it the role of the NACWC, and her duty as legislative chairman, "to emphasize the necessity of doing one's duty to her country, her State and the city or town in which she lives by learning all she can about the practical situation and then doing everything in her power to have wise, just laws enacted." Unlike Bethune, Terrell believed the best way to achieve these aims was to "put just men into positions of responsibility and power." Terrell did not think talking about and focusing so relentlessly on women was the best use of the organization's political time. She said it was instead the group's duty to "have the right type of men nominated for the various offices" and "urge their representatives to vote for bills which will help improve our condition as a race." Black women, Terrell thought, had a duty to support Black male leaders. She did not think women should strike out on their own and assume leadership positions with a national profile.[12]

Bethune strongly disagreed. She insisted that the NACWC was no longer a group whose primary mission was ensuring that Black men receive the first pick of jobs, but rather, one that sought to include women in the category of "citizen" in the United States and to lobby Congress on all bills "affecting the ECONOMIC, SOCIAL, MORAL and POLITICAL WELFARE of citizens" (emphasis hers) and advise them on how to secure the passage or defeat of these bills. As historian Joyce Hanson has shown, to ensure Terrell would not undermine this prime directive, Bethune inserted a clause in the charge to the committee saying that the organization's Legislative Department, which Terrell directed, would no longer be free to make its own determinations about such things and, going forward, would have to submit any legislative plans to the president of the NACWC for approval. This new directive bypassed Terrell and stripped her of a large amount of her legislative discretion. Bethune said this was a necessary change because she wanted their organization to openly support several bills then before Congress. These included the Dyer Anti-Lynching Bill, the Child Labor Amendment, which would improve the work lives of Black children, and the bill to establish a World Court tied to the League of Nations. Bethune thought this last was important because it could create a world judicial body to which Black people could appeal for a ruling regarding crimes perpetrated against their humanity. Bethune believed women's organizations now needed to take a leadership role in addressing issues of national and international concern. A women's organization could, she believed, be at the forefront of lobbying for and addressing issues relevant to all Black people, not just women.[13]

Given the tensions around her leadership vision, it was only a matter of time before Bethune determined that she would need a completely new organization to accomplish her goals. On December 5, 1935, Bethune called together thirty women for a meeting at the West 137th Street branch of the YWCA in New York City. The women were the leading representatives of national education, health, nursing, religious, fraternal, business, and racial organizations. Bethune's goal was to win their support for the launch of the National Council of Negro Women (NCNW), an "organization comprised of organizations." Each group would remain sovereign and continue to hold to its own guiding principles and practices, but all organizations, twenty-six in total, would commit to coming together as needed to form a united front. As Bethune summarized her vision,

> The National Council of Negro Women has as its aim the bringing together of the Negro race for the united effort in the things where we need to be united. It does not aim to stand in the way of the program of any individual organization, but to pool our interests, in order to be able to show the activities of Negro women in this country wherever pressure is needed, on whatever

needs to come together for the opening of doors for our group.[14]

Though the high-profile members of the NACWC agreed that the organization would join this new entity, behind the scenes, the derision, second-guessing, and charges that Bethune was drunk on the wine of hubris flowed hot and heavy.

The representatives of the twenty-six Black women's groups initially invited to attend the gathering discussed the possibility of forming a permanent "council" that would meet regularly and solidify their role as a force to be reckoned with in legislative matters impacting Black people in the United States. Bethune appealed to the women to expand their horizons by thinking "of the big things done by past leadership who dared to stand for right and let us fight today with Negro womanhood in mind." Though the majority of women at the NCNW's founding meeting were enthusiastic and supported Bethune's proposal wholeheartedly, some of her closest allies did not believe there was much reason to start another organization for Black women when, as far as they were concerned, one already existed, the NACWC. Charlotte Hawkins Brown, a close friend of Bethune's, publicly supported the idea of the new organization, but then wrote to other club women, saying the idea was "air castle building and dreaming." Mary Church Terrell wrote back that she agreed and "did not see how the mistakes made by other groups will not be made by this one." Still, in a show of unity, the women voted unanimously to establish the NCNW, and Terrell insisted that the women cast a unanimous ballot for Bethune as president. Bethune, always the strategist, was aware of the private resistance to her and her ideas. Determined to press forward, she decided that she would "keep her enemies close," as they say, and incorporated some of her detractors in prominent positions in the new organization.[15]

In April 1936, the NCNW held its first conference, to adopt a constitution and elect permanent officers. Dress and fashion returned as an issue, but this time the concerns had to do with the members in attendance, not hand-wringing about lower-class Black people shaming their upper-class sisters. On day one, the membership showed up fashionably attired, some wearing "hats and mink coats and fancy dresses" and spent the first few days seemingly more concerned with their wardrobe changes than in attending the working sessions. A parade of women left the room in one outfit and then returned sometime later in a different ensemble. Bethune quickly tired of the "fashion show" atmosphere of the conference, including ladies strolling up and down aisles following a clothing change. By the second day of the meeting, she was truly frustrated and, as attendee Henrine Ward Banks recalled, addressed the group to say,

> Ladies, I am going to tell you something. Take off your hats. Let's leave the mink coats in the back. Let's roll up our sleeves and get ready to go to work. I am putting someone on the doors. And you are not to leave the building. We will go downstairs to lunch—we will not leave the building for lunch. We will close our meeting at five. You will have plenty of time to go back and put on your evening dresses and go to dinner.[16]

We do not know how the speech went over among those in attendance, or anything about who was put "on the doors" to try to stop the women from leaving and changing clothes. I wish we did.

As the years passed, the group's agenda coalesced around the issues of segregation, lynching, voter education, public housing, education, job training, civil service reform, consumer rights, public health, expansion of Social Security benefits, and equity in social welfare programs. Voting remained a central focus. Instead of merely registering Black people to vote and engaging in what amounted to get-out-the-vote campaigns, the NCNW pioneered a decentralized and innovative "citizenship program" that began with any women who were interested in getting out the vote also agreeing to first study their state constitutions and voting laws so they would know what issues would most especially speak to Black women. In addition, across the country, locally based members of the NCNW offered workshops to teach women how to use a voting machine or mark a ballot. NCNW members also urged Black women to choose to become active in local political organizations that addressed issues they found most pressing in their own communities. Building on that local focus, NCNW activists urged women to study and publicize the voting records of local, state, and national officials, be they positive or negative, as a way of developing criteria for supporting one candidate over another. Some chapters had members draw up petitions to advocate for specific community issues and to take the further step of presenting those petitions at public hearings or dropping them off at the local offices of their government representatives. Overall, the "citizenship program" taught that women should strive to be intelligent and engaged members of the electorate.[17]

The group was also interested in having an impact at the federal level. That is how it came to be that in April 1938, with the support of her longtime friend and ally Eleanor Roosevelt, Bethune was able to bring the work of the NCNW's citizenship program to the notice of officials in the federal government. Roosevelt organized a meeting for sixty-five members of the NCNW with several government officials in the East Room of the White House. By all accounts, the discussion was dominated by Bethune, who called on the officials present to appoint "qualified Negro women" who "are in closer touch with the problems of their own group" to administrative positions in the Children's Bureau, Bureau of Public Health, Women's Bureau of the US Department of Labor, Bureau of Education, Federal Housing Administration, and the Social Security Board. The women had done their research and knew that those agencies and groups had no such representation and, as Bethune argued, were the departments and agencies having an outsize impact on the lives of Black people in the United States. It's not clear that any of the agencies responded particularly forcefully to her requests, but Bethune definitely used the occasion to make clear to all with ears to hear that the NCNW was serious about developing the political power of Black women.[18]

The same year Bethune and her NCNW compatriots held their first organizing meeting, 1935, Bethune was just beginning a role in FDR's New Deal administration as director of Negro Affairs in the National Youth Administration (NYA), a division of the Works Progress Administration. As was true with all her political work, in this role she continued to champion Black women and children.

The Depression had drastically disrupted educational and employment opportunities of more than twenty million young people between the ages of sixteen and twenty-five who were poor and working class and could ill afford to be without either. Unsurprisingly, the largest impact fell on Black people in the rural South. As a way of helping all young people, the organization first created work-study funds for any students between sixteen and twenty-five who wanted to continue their education but needed financial support to do so. Bethune wanted to ensure that young Black people were able to benefit as well, including targeted support for Black women and girls. In one of her first acts in the role of director, she created "five special camps for Negro girls" and located them in New Jersey, North and South Carolina, Florida, and Arkansas. Unlike the majority of other such camps created during the period, which were mostly for white children, the Bethune NYA Camps were specifically for unemployed single Black women between eighteen and twenty-five. In addition to helping the students and young people who came to the camps, Bethune struck a deal to locate them on the campuses of Black colleges and universities, financially benefiting those institutions.[19]

In keeping with Bethune's commitment to public health, the staff at all the camps included a camp physician and nurse, providing health care to young people who rarely had regular access to it. The vocational classes offered a stipend to students of six dollars per day, the same rate that white students received. Additional activities included student government associations, to teach skills in civics; a camp newspaper, the *Bethune Spotlight*, that helped to teach writing skills; a lecture series where students learned about Black history and achievement; and a picture gallery of accomplished Black women. In addition, according to a 2014 article written by an archivist at the National Archives named Jametta Davis, the NYA's Special Negro Fund provided educational aid and work-study programs to Black college students, which allowed young women to "remain in college, acquire additional job skills, and participate in paid projects providing opportunities to instruct and assist other NYA participants in the various vocational programs." The NYA also collaborated with local schools, hospitals, and organizations "such as the YWCA to provide them with training in nursery school work, home economics, gardening, cafeteria work, nursing, clerical skills, and factory work." The program also created a number of residential training centers on and near the campuses of Black colleges so that the selected girls could travel to the centers and reside for extended periods as they learned new trades and skills. These young women all earned wages for their part-time work.

The impact of these programs was multifaceted and significant. Nonetheless, political pressure to stop funding programs for Black people and communities at the same level as those for whites forced the closure of the camps and first to a slowing and then a halt to the other work as well. In the end, the NYA assisted close to three hundred thousand Black youth. They could not claim to have ended poverty or unemployment for Black people, but they certainly paved the way for thousands of young Black women to earn much-needed money while having access to workforce training that enabled them to have better job opportunities. The NYA was ended in 1943, and with it, Bethune's formal government service.

Bethune dreamed of a world where Black women and girls basked in the warmth of their collective suns. To create it, this place of sunlight, safety, and community, she strategized a future and dreamed a world order that included those who worked in domestic service, elite Black people who employed Black domestic servants, and everyone in between. The thread she pulled to encircle the whole was the fact of Blackness and the ways its folds draped, lay, and shaped how Black women learned, earned, and survived the world. In her mind's eye, she saw a bridge in need of building, and crossing it offered paths for Black women everywhere to discover a way to find one another and build freedom together as

communities of the willing linked arms and showed committed strength and resolve as they marched toward progress,
peace, and survival. As audacious as it was unprecedented,
an agenda of such depth and breadth required, Bethune
thought, institutions such as schools and organizations, a
clear agenda, and strategies previously unimagined. She
was like a traveler gathering tools and inspiration for the
journey. As a young woman, she saw education as the path to
power and influence. Then, as a more mature woman, she
joined and remade organizations before becoming a figure
who redirected the resources of the federal government to
benefit Black women. At the end of her life, she was a woman
in solidarity with other women in a global fight against patri-
archy and colonization. If my twelve-year-old self marveled
at the world Toni Morrison created in *The Bluest Eye,* the
adult version of who I am appreciates Bethune's angle of vision and understanding about the nature and purpose of
politics, organizing, and strategies aimed at helping Black
women find calm if not complete safety in turbulent political, social, and cultural seas. Bethune did not believe there
was one road to be trod to a land called freedom. There were
multiple paths worth exploring. She thought that the least
treacherous path forward for the largest number of Black
women was to join together and become an organized body
too large and powerful to fail. Over the arc of her political

career, she shifted strategies and tactics, but she never failed to move toward the light of her one true truth and mission: including Black people in the polity of the United States on terms that they could live with, and not die from. She wanted Black women to have the chance to lead the way.

5

BLACK: CAPITAL,
CAPITALISM,
AND RELAXATION

This is a story of capital, capitalism, and the knife's edge walked by the sons and daughters of the enslaved who believed the tools capitalism teaches could lead Black people to freedom. It is about Bethune, her ancestors, and a beach named Bethune. It is about a man named Abraham Lincoln Lewis and the beach he founded and named American. It is about his ancestors, and their understanding that Black survival was bound up with a kind of relaxation that provided salvation beyond rest. It is about the tenderness wrought by believing children could and should scream lustily because of their joy, and not their pain. It is about Amelia Island, a piece of land surrounded by water, some of it of the fresh river variety but most of it a salted sea. This is about the shared understanding that for a people struggling not to drown in the rising tides of fascism, exclusion, and exploitation, there is a way for Black capital to defeat the terrors of capitalism in the cause of Black freedom. These beaches tell a story about a group of people who understood the why of creating, seeking out, and embracing the relief of a jaw unclenching at the sound of waves rolling fast toward them. They knew the truth, reality, and beauty of a tickle of sweat trickling down foreheads, breasts, and chests as hips find a shared rhythm and bodies swaying in community refine a collective beat.

The businesspeople, political activists, and "just folks" who built American Beach said they did so because they needed a place where all Black people—those who had money, those making it from one paycheck to the next, and those struggling to consistently earn a steady livelihood—could experience community together. The goal was to use Black capital to repudiate the violence of capitalism so often directed at Black people. They wanted to build Black wealth, promote Black joy, and forge Black community. I know this island and this beach. My grandparents owned a home there in community with Black people who began building it in 1935. It existed because racism and white supremacy existed, because by the 1920s, laws in Florida banned Black people from most of the beaches in the state. Those who built American Beach said they did so because they needed a place where they and theirs could experience, as the community motto stated, "Relaxation and Recreation without Humiliation."

American Beach's primary founder, Abraham Lincoln Lewis, was born two months after his namesake signed the Emancipation Proclamation in 1865 and was one of the founding partners of the Afro-American Industrial and Benefit Association, Florida's first Black insurance company. The company was destroyed in the Great Jacksonville Fire of 1901, and Lewis rebuilt it, becoming the first manager of the association, which was renamed the Afro-American Insurance Company. Mary McLeod Bethune sold life insurance policies for the company for five years as she struggled to make ends meet in Palatka, Florida, where she ministered to prisoners while trying to start a school. In 1919, Lewis became president of the Afro-American Insurance Company, and as a means of utilizing Black capital to finance Black self-sufficiency and life, in the 1920s, he authorized the company to begin providing mortgages for individual homes in the Jacksonville area. In 1929 he built the Lincoln Golf and Country Club, a golf course where Black celebrities from around the country came to play the game, eat, and socialize. In 1935, in the depths of the Depression, he was instrumental in the creation of American Beach. Bethune, by then a political force in her own right, was a member of the company's board of directors. She participated when the insurance company's pension department used the funds it had accumulated to buy thirty-three acres on Amelia Island with one thousand feet of beach fronting the Atlantic Ocean. The company acquired two other parcels later—the final one in 1945 in the form of a grant from the US government under President Harry Truman that Mary McLeod Bethune arranged and facilitated. The whole became American Beach.[1]

That beach, death by drowning, space and time, and the souls of Black people are entangled at that very spot and have been for a very long time. I was there, in the state of Florida, at the place called American Beach, on an island named Amelia the day death came looking for me. I was about nine and had recently learned to swim in an outdoor pool at the YWCA. I had great confidence in my floating, and breath holding, and even opening my eyes underwater. At some point as I splashed in ocean water deep enough to lift my feet from the bottom and float, but close enough to the shore that my grandparents could easily see my bright yellow rubber beach cap bob, I turned onto my back to practice floating. I stared up at and beyond the blue-white sky and dreamed a bit as the waves rocked, joining me and sky in a perfect quiet motion. I did not notice trouble had found me until, instead of rocking, there was pulling and pushing as an undertow, or riptide, or the current announced itself. All water is by nature wet, but it does not all have the same temperament. I had only practiced swimming and floating in a peaceful pool where safety was the feel of cement only ever a few kicks away. I knew nothing of this living thing I had to fight to stay above. That's when I began to feel a tugging, almost like hands pushing me out farther, or maybe it was down. Everything that had been warm and comforting and peaceful changed as I was sucked toward something or somewhere I knew I did not want to be but was not strong enough to stop. I tried to go back the way I had come, but as I imagine is true of the suck of quicksand, the more I fought to impose my will, the faster I went in the wrong direction. I tried to swim underwater, but I couldn't see anything, and the ocean closing over my head felt wrong and terrifying. Panic jerked me, terror pounded my insides. Then I remembered, or felt, or just knew that if I couldn't go back, and didn't want to go forward, I'd best try to go sideways, to swim parallel to the shore instead of toward or away from it. I later learned that was the exact right way to fight an unfriendly current.

When I walked up out of the sea and collapsed on the

white sand and stared at the same blue-white sky that had so recently betrayed me, I knew whatever had held me in that water had decided on its own to let me go. I had not bested it. It had released me connected to souls across time and space by fear, forces beyond my control, and the sea. I later learned that over hundreds of years, thousands of Black people died in those waters. That form of Black death began during the slave trade when the captains of such ships hurled their still living cargo overboard to escape prosecution for engaging in the outlawed trafficking of human beings. For those so murdered, only a small number of their limp, bloated, soulless bodies ever touched land again. Those that did floated up right where I had stumbled out of the sea. When MaVynee Betsch, known to all at the time as the Beach Lady, told me the story, she said those chained and drowned dead Africans sometimes called on the living to join them. One child and four adults drowned, and six others came close at that same spot on one single day in 1994 when the sea was particularly hungry for company. That was more dead at one time than the ocean had coughed up for many, many years.[2] The presence of the drowned dead was so well-known a feature of American Beach that a writer named Nikesha Elise Williams described it and its relation to disposable human cargo in a 2020 article for *The Bitter Southerner*. She wrote, "This murky history lesson into the annals and underbelly of

America's beginning is vital to the story of American Beach because, as its denizens and defenders often note, there is magic, healing, and a certain energy in its waters. They attribute this alchemy to ancestors whose souls still speak from their watery graves to those willing to listen." Malcolm Jackson, a photographer who lives in Jacksonville, Florida, and who regularly photographs Black people at American Beach, says, "You get a certain type of spiritual vibration there when we go to that beach, especially during the sunset. It just feels as if the slaves are calling to you."[3]

So it is that oral historians of the community declared the place I stumbled up and out of the water to be haunted by the souls of dead Africans drowned by slavers. After the United States outlawed the importation of new slaves in 1807, slave traders from New England and elsewhere simply registered their ships under the Spanish flag. At the time, Florida was, and for several more decades would remain, a Spanish colony where slavery was legal. So, US-owned Spanish-registered slave ships simply brought their illegal cargo of Africans to a warehouse in the town of Fernandina before smuggling them a few hours north to Georgia for sale. Because the penalty for continuing to engage in the slave trade was death by hanging, when these vessels were approached by authorities demanding to inspect their cargo holds, the captain and crew threw Africans overboard to drown. When I first heard this history, as the horror of it bloomed, moving hot and aching through me, in defense, I began to dream of a Black Atlantis where instead of dying a flailing, gasping, choking, and chained death, some spontaneously developed the capacity to breathe and live underwater where they could be free. I have no reason to believe that is true. I have no proof it is not.[4]

6

ON THE SOIL AND IN THE NAME OF ONE'S ANCESTORS

Amelia Island is sometimes referred to as the Isle of Eight Flags. Given that the Indigenous people who had long lived in the area did not mark their territory in that manner, the flag from France was the first to snap in the island's wind. This was after Jean Ribault landed there in 1562 and named the island Isle de Mar. Just a few years later, in 1565, Spain invaded with troops under the command of Pedro Menendez de Aviles. After defeating the French, the Spanish conquerors renamed the island Isla de Santa María and unfurled flag number two. The next European country to prevail was Britain; James Oglethorpe gave it the name that stuck, Amelia Island. He did so to honor King George's daughter while negotiating the island's transfer from Spain to Britain in 1763. The Spanish weren't done, however, and during the American Revolutionary War, Spain cooperated with colonists against the British. As a reward, Amelia Island was gifted to them, and they again flew the Spanish flag over the territory.

In 1812, the Patriots of Amelia Island seized control of the island during the Seminole Wars, when Indigenous and Black people fought the US Army. They raised the Patriot Flag, which was flag number four. Spain again took over the island in 1813, and a few years later, in 1817, a Scottish-born South American named Gregor MacGregor seized and claimed the island for "the brethren of Mexico, Buenos Aires, New Granada and Venezuela." The flag they flew had a green cross on it, and was the fifth to claim ownership. Soon, though, Spanish soldiers forced MacGregor's withdrawal from the island. But once again, the Spanish troops could not prevail and soon surrendered the island to the French privateer Louis-Michel Aury, who was fighting on behalf of Mexico. When he sailed his ships into the harbor, though French by birth, Aury raised the Mexican flag. This was number six. The seventh was the US flag: America took control of the territory from Spain in 1821. That lasted until the Civil War broke out in 1861 when Amelia Island was under the Confederate States of America flag. This was the eighth flag to fly over the island.[1]

Once Florida was again part of the United States, it was,

as was most of the South, a slave state. That changed in 1865 with the conclusion of the Civil War and the declaration of victory by the Union Army. The story of Black freedom and the saga of Black land ownership began then, when General William T. Sherman issued Special Field Order No. 15. This order declared that the coastline stretching from Charleston, South Carolina, to the St. Johns River in Florida was to be given to newly freed Black people. With the stroke of that pen, Sherman's order redistributed almost four hundred thousand acres of land to forty thousand newly freed Black families, in forty-acre segments. In addition to land, the order made clear, "On the islands, and in the settlements hereafter to be established, no white person whatever, unless military officers and soldiers detailed for duty, will be permitted to reside; and the sole and exclusive management of affairs will be left to the freed people themselves, subject only to the United States military authority and the acts of Congress." Those who were able to get land for themselves were determined to use their skills and labor to make the land productive. The Black people who moved to those islands, including Amelia Island, set up their own civic and educational institutions and established their own militia to protect themselves from the Klan and other white supremacist organizations. In a later order, Sherman authorized the army to loan mules to the newly settled farmers so they could provide for themselves in what he imagined would be a segregated Black homeland. Things went well for a bit. A radical plan for land redistribution in the South, enacted by a single order, by a single man, Sherman's field order was designed to simultaneously punish Confederate planters along the coast, who had been particularly vigorous in their support of the Civil War, and aid Black people who had little means of caring for themselves. At least initially, the plan garnered support. Congressional leaders convinced President Lincoln to establish the Bureau of Refugees, Freedmen, and Abandoned Lands, known as the Freedmen's Bureau, as a way of administering the process. However, that outcome was short-lived; following Lincoln's assassination, the new president, Andrew Johnson, overturned Sherman's directive in the fall of 1865 and returned most of the land along the South Carolina, Georgia, and Florida coasts to the former plantation owners.[2]

In 1933, just a few years before Abraham Lincoln Lewis and the executives in his company decided to use the money in the company's pension fund to build American Beach, the federal government established the Home Owners' Loan Corporation (HOLC) to expand homeownership for white people as part of their effort to help the nation recover from the Great Depression. To determine mortgage-worthiness, HOLC created maps of at least 239 US cities, using high numbers of white people in a community as a positive measure, and large numbers of Black ones as a negative. To make clear how central racial composition would be, staff working for the government agency literally drew red lines around communities with large Black populations as a way of marking them as unsuitable for investment. Black people within those communities would not receive HOLC loans; over generations this deprived Black communities of homeownership, central for intergenerational wealth transfer. This one government-sanctioned practice validated other racist maneuvers, such as restrictive covenants that barred Black people from homeownership by means of legal agreements set up by previous owners, by undervaluing real estate in Black neighborhoods, and by mob violence against Black people who moved into white neighborhoods. Those who did manage to own property often found that white elected officials and civil servants used their authority to levy outrageously high taxes on their property, or that rules and regulations were suddenly changed to disadvantage Black people who sought to engage the supposed American ideals of hard work bringing financial and societal rewards.[3]

Decades before the US government began to use its resources to make home ownership available to white people, Lewis devised a plan to utilize Black capital to jumpstart Black homeownership. He took his first step in 1919. According to

Russ Rymer, a journalist who spent a year living on the island, writing a book about its history and significance, Lewis's first efforts, like many similar efforts in the United States, focused disproportionally on providing leisure opportunities to wealthy Black people. The first group to benefit from American Beach were the executives of the life insurance company and other wealthy Black people who could afford it. Beginning in 1940, the company offered lots for sale to any Black people who could pay the $150 fee to purchase a buildable lot. As Rymer describes it, at that point, American Beach took on a decidedly "democratic caste"—a maid might own a home next to an executive. This community-building model and the financing available to those wanting to purchase into it was particularly important after World War II, when home construction and ownership took off. Here, much as in the 1930s, government policies excluded Black people. The GI Bill was supposed to ensure that housing, education, and even resources for business creation were available for qualified veterans. Initially, Black veterans could not participate. By 1950, the Federal Housing Administration and the Veterans Administration together insured half of all new home mortgages in the US, and both used race as a criterion, not only for individual mortgages but also in the financing of entire subdivisions. Once again, as in the 1930s, government policies disadvantaged Black people and privileged American citizens whose skin was white.[4]

Lewis, Bethune, and all the others associated with American Beach determined to strike a blow for Black self-determination; their weapons would be land, community, and rest. American Beach was never just about a place to swim or a home to buy. It was an audacious experiment in segregation and community as a weapon to empower. It all ended in 1964 when a hurricane named Dora knocked down much of what was there and then, by 1968, integration made a segregated beach community passé for a younger generation who ran headlong into the homes, communities, and schools white America had long denied them.[5]

Though American Beach is today a remnant of what it had once been, it still exists and Black people still own homes there, though there are almost as many mansions and millionaires as there are modest homes hugging the land low and hard. My father and I sold the house his parents, my grandparents, built there once the taxes got too high for me, a graduate student, and him, a retiree on a fixed income. The family we sold it to turned it into an Airbnb, and I have returned to stay there. It's like an echo of the house I remember. When my husband first met my father, it was there at the beach. The two of them spent their first few hours of knowing each other replacing all the windows in the bright pink single-story cement home. Those windows remain today. My bedroom is the same. The bedroom my great-grandmother slept in is still there, as is the original though updated bathroom. That part still feels, smells, seems familiar. There is now a fancy new kitchen, the screened-in porch is now a dining room, and there is a second floor that is basically a bedroom and bathroom. But it is at its core still the house I grew up in. What drew me back to it was the opportunity to talk with the one person I knew who revered Bethune and American Beach in equal measure. Her name is Johnnetta Cole. Though she had a long and distinguished career as an anthropologist before I met her, I first made her acquaintance when I was an undergraduate at Spelman College. After a vigorous protest by students dismayed that the board of trustees seemed poised to choose another man for the role of president, Dr. Cole was selected to serve as the first Black woman president of the school. I have a picture of her with me at my graduation ceremony. I treasure it. I called her my president, and madame president, in a "my president, Johnnetta Cole, said" kind of way for quite a bit. It was years later that I learned we had American Beach in common. A. L. Lewis was her great-grandfather and Mary McLeod Bethune was someone she described to me as being one of her earliest mentors. When we talked, she had earlier that week just stepped down as the president of the National Council of Negro Women, the Black women's organization Bethune started. She was in her mideighties and was nearing the end of a home-building process on American Beach, where she was planning to live out her days.

I began the conversation by asking her to tell me about her family and what grounded her, kept her centered. She told me: "You know where I come from in a literal sense. I come from Jacksonville, Florida. I come from American Beach. I come from Abraham Lincoln (A. L.) Lewis. This man had faith and fortitude!" She described his birth in 1865 and migration to Jacksonville and his founding of the Afro-American Insurance Company along with six other Black men. This, she said, was the first Black insurance company in the state of Florida. He went on to become the first Black millionaire there. He was, Cole murmured, "a race man and he had an extraordinary relationship with a race woman named Dr. Mary McLeod Bethune." Bethune was a member of the board of Edward Waters College, which was founded by Lewis because, she said, "he asked her to," and Lewis sat on the board of Bethune-Cookman, the college Bethune founded, because she asked him to. Dr. Cole recalled that when she was quite young, her mother would sometimes drive her and her sister down to Daytona Beach, about one hour and thirty minutes away, to visit friends, and if Dr. Bethune was in her office, they would sit or play while listening to the grown-ups talk. She added, "When I have respectfully said she was one of my earliest mentors, there is truth to it."[6]

American Beach was a Black community started by race men and women who were not just interested in selling leisure, or becoming real estate developers cultivating a Black market, or even an enclave where wealthy Black people could socialize with "their sort of people," she told me. It was a dream based on community as both shield and weapon that withstood for a bit, but then, for lack of others willing to pick up the torch and carry it forward, couldn't continue to burn as brightly as it once had. I asked her to explain this term, "race men and race women," and to tell me why it was important in relation to American Beach. She said the most important thing to know was that as she was growing up, she and her siblings were taught that they were responsible, not just for themselves but for others. Especially if you were wealthy, she said, it was supposed to be your responsibility to make sure Black people as a group, across class, had the structural support and spiritual nourishment to not only survive but to thrive and grow strong together. She said she also grew up hearing the saying "From those to whom much has been given, much is required." And so, one of the fundamental values she said was instilled in her was that she had no choice but to be of service to others, not just of service to herself. She added, "Those ideas were all around me, in the church, in schools and in Black organizations. It was all around me. And so, I grew up in a family of race women and men, and I was told, I dare not break the chain."[7]

Though she moved, worked, and sometimes lived among white people, Bethune, as a race woman, also believed in Black businesses and in keeping Black dollars circulating in Black communities. One of her biographers, Rackham Holt, says Bethune told her about an unemployed veteran who was trying to figure out an income stream to support him and his family and was having some difficulty securing anything promising. Bethune suggested he think about becoming an entrepreneur and offered to give him what in our day would amount to "start-up funds" to buy a wagon, an ice pick, and a block of ice so he could begin a business selling ice for iceboxes. Then she took the step of putting the word out around Daytona's Black community, asking everyone to support their community member and his new business instead of the white gentleman who was then the lone seller of ice in the area and so had a monopoly on their business. A few weeks later, Bethune checked back in to ask the newly minted ice seller how his new career was going. He said he had more business than he could keep up with and was planning to buy an actual cart to replace the wagon and thought he might get his son to go into business with him. He thanked Bethune both for the loan and for asking the community to support him, and proudly repaid the money she had loaned him. During the exchange, he mentioned that there was only one person in the community who had declined to purchase his ice and continued to purchase from the white ice seller. He told Bethune who the person was, and she went over to the lone holdout and out of curiosity asked why she had made that choice. She said, "I tried the Black man's ice, but the white man's ice was colder." She is an example of how not to be a race woman.[8]

When Dr. Cole's great-grandfather A. L. Lewis died in 1947, he was a member of the board for another beach town with a similar dream. That one was located in Volusia County, about forty-five minutes from Daytona Beach, where Bethune had founded her school. This one was founded by Mary Mc-Leod Bethune; it was known as Bethune Beach. Bethune Beach's creation story was completely different from American Beach's. Lacking the capital to purchase land outright, and not able to get her friends and supporters in the government to gift her any property, Bethune's beach project began as a Black dream infused with Black wealth but ended up running into white resistance. To raise the initial capital, Bethune turned to people she knew and with whom she had long worked. There was Garfield Devoe Rogers, one of her cofounders in the Central Life Insurance Company. Rogers assumed the presidency in 1935 and led the company to almost a million dollars in assets in the next few years. In a 1943 article for *American Mercury* magazine about the statewide meeting of the Negro Defense Committee, the writer and anthropologist Zora Neale Hurston quoted him as saying: "The only citizens who count are those who give time, effort, and money to the support and growth of the community. Share the burden where you live." Another of Bethune Beach's initial investors was Nathaniel "Professor" Crooms, who in 1926 founded a secondary "academy" in Sanford, Florida, for Black students, which was among the first to offer college preparatory classes. The last of the investors was Lawrence Silas, a successful cattleman in Osceola, whom Bethune's son, Albert, described as one of his mother's "major" if silent financial backers. With the initial funding in place, all they needed was the beachfront property.

In 1943, Bethune convinced a wealthy developer friend she knew to sell her a two-and-a-half-mile stretch of beachfront property in Volusia County, south of Daytona. The mortgage on the property was $132,000, more than $2 million today. Not having a company pension plan to underwrite the project, her first order of business was to try to convince Black people to buy into the development. Bethune took to the press to announce the opportunity: "For a long time the progressive citizens of America have recognized the strategic value of a beach resort on the Atlantic Coast owned and controlled by Negroes." She added, "Those of us who sincerely believe that recreation is essential to the good life should be encouraged to know that in the deep South great strides are being made."[9] While Bethune worked to build enthusiasm for Bethune Beach publicly, the group privately found that they had to dig deeply into their own pockets to keep their dream of the Black resort alive. They had to pay to have the land cleared, some of the roads cut, and water and sewage services connected to the property as white county officials stalled or outright refused to provide the development with services. In a 2014 interview, Albert put the figure the group had to spend at roughly $200,000. This was just one of the obstacles the founders of Bethune Beach had to overcome. The history of violence associated with the place was another.[10]

Bethune would have had to work hard to convince Black people to travel to that part of central Florida, as it was known for being vehemently anti-Black and dangerous. Just a few years before, in 1939, Bethune spoke out about a lynching in Daytona, the city in which Bethune-Cookman was located. The victim was named Lee Snell. Mr. Snell was a veteran who had returned from World War I and purchased a car he outfitted as a taxi. He was driving in the early-morning hours when Benny Blackwelder, a twelve-year-old white child on a bicycle, darted out in front of the taxi. The impact killed the child. The police officers summoned to the scene initially declared the death an unfortunate accident and released Mr. Snell, who returned home. Later that afternoon, the constable, James Durden, showed up to take Mr. Snell into custody, telling him he was going to have to take him in on manslaughter charges. Before the two men traveled very far, they were forced to stop when they came upon a barricade in the road manned by Benny Blackwelder's two older brothers, Everett and Earl. For some reason, when faced with the two armed men, the constable decided the best way to calm the brothers and keep the prisoner safe was to remove him from the safety of the car. Though he was handcuffed, the two brothers immediately began to beat, kick, and pistol-whip Mr. Snell. Constable Durden said he feared for his life and so could not intervene, but he later said that at some point in the beating, Mr. Snell broke free and tried to "escape." The brothers opened fire on the bound, bloodied, and beaten man. One shot him in the leg, the other shot him in the back and continued to fire while sauntering closer and closer to the dead man. When Constable Durden was first interviewed about what had taken place, he said Mr. Snell's death was "cold-blooded murder" and he identified the two men he had seen do it. Besides Constable Durden, at least six other motorists witnessed the murder. Mr. Snell's body was taken to a local funeral home, but the owners feared further violence was to come when the coroner requested to view Mr. Snell's body as part of their investigation. The officials of the funeral home expressed deep reservations, saying they were "afraid it might be stolen and dragged around the streets," as was common during the era when mobs and spectators degraded the bodies of the victims of racial terror. These mobs sometimes left them on display, dragged them through public areas, and even took souvenirs from their remains.[11]

Initially, the county made no attempts to locate or apprehend the Blackwelder brothers, but eventually, Everett and Earl Blackwelder turned themselves in to the sheriff. Based on Constable Durden's testimony and other eyewitness accounts, the coroner's jury returned a verdict that Lee Snell's death was the result of "murder at the hands of Earl and Everett Blackwelder." The Blackwelder brothers waived a preliminary hearing, entered a plea of innocence before the local justice of the peace, and were held without bail in the county jail. That was the only time they would spend in jail. Though Constable Durden had been willing at first to offer his eyewitness account and testimony concerning the guilt of the Blackwelder brothers, when the court trial began, he recanted his earlier identification, stating that he "thought" but wasn't sure Earl and Everett Blackwelder were the men responsible for murdering Lee Snell. Now he said he "might have been mistaken" and that he had been "under great mental strain" when he gave his deposition. Given this waffling, the circuit court jury returned a verdict acquitting the Blackwelder brothers of all charges. In the end, no one was held accountable for Mr. Snell's murder, which took place in broad daylight with seven people watching, including Constable Durden. Given that another lynching of another Black man had taken place in Panama City, Florida, a few weeks before Mr. Snell's, under similar circumstances, the lynching of Lee Snell attracted state and national attention.[12]

Mary McLeod Bethune wrote to the president of the United States, to other friends and supporters, and to local white people with power to ask that something be done. She also wrote a letter to the editors of Daytona Beach's newspaper to ask for justice for Mr. Snell, saying, "Citizens of Volusia County, and of the State of Florida, the eyes of America and the world are turned this way, taking note of your standard of justice. We are crushed but we are not discouraged."[13]

This was a different kind of historical violence than that haunting American Beach, with its stories of murdered Africans persisting over centuries, but the ways violence haunted the memories of Black people in and around Bethune Beach was equally strong. Land sold to Black people sometimes has to be cleansed of the blood of Black innocents as surely as the memories of murder must be expunged from Black psyches. There can be no cure for terror that does not involve space, breath, peace, and safety. Bethune wanted the resort town to be a space where Black residents could congregate in the sun and sand without, flyers for the development proclaimed, "the fear of harassment." Taking a page from American Beach's book, she touted Black ownership and community as an important part of the story. Though all were welcomed on the beach, the marker posted to commemorate the history of what Bethune created said that home and business ownership was to remain in Black hands. It wasn't just Black relaxation she and her cofounders were after; they wanted to support Black land and home ownership.[14]

For the first few years of Bethune Beach's existence, the only house built on the property was pink. The owners, Hilder Davie and his wife, purchased the land and built the house after he dreamed of his deceased father one night and awoke the next morning recalling a number his father had handed him. Believing it was a sign, he gathered all the money he had saved and that his relatives would lend him and placed a bet with the Cuban Lottery/Bolita. His bet paid off to the tune of $40,000. He invested his winnings heavily in real estate in the Miami area, building a house and purchasing an apartment building as an investment. At the insistent urging of his wife, Barbara, he also bought property at Bethune Beach, paid to have the road put in, and built the home in which they relocated for long stretches of time.[15] That one early success was not readily followed by others willing and able to purchase property and build a house. Given the mortgage and tax payments hanging over Bethune Beach, and the lack of capital to underwrite mortgages, Bethune was forced to try to rely on an exploitative and precarious financing scheme known as installment contracts to get people to buy into the project. An installment contract, today known as a balloon mortgage, is an arrangement where the buyer agrees to pay to the seller the purchase price plus interest in installments over a set period of time. The buyer is immediately able to take possession of the property, but if they miss any of their monthly payments, they have to forfeit the property and all the money they had invested. One example of how this all worked at Bethune Beach, and the daunting challenges to successful homeownership for Black people, is found in an August 2021 newspaper article by Francis Wilkinson about an eighty-nine-year-old Bethune Beach property owner named Hester Bland. During the course of the interview, Bland described what it took for her to become a property owner, first in Miami, and then at Bethune Beach. She said that first and foremost, she took every possible opportunity to work extra jobs, telling Wilkinson:

> When summertime came and the kids got out of school, I went to school, picked them up and took them directly to the train station. I had their bags already packed; their lunches packed. I put them on the train and sent them to grandma for three months. So, for three months I was able to work two jobs. I'd work at the hospital, give them eight-and-a-half hours. Then I'd leave and go to a nursing home and work for another eight-and-a-half hours, until 11.

After years of keeping up this pace, Bland and her husband were able to save enough for a down payment on a home. The developer who sold it to them gave the couple a five-year interest-only mortgage, much like the loans mortgage companies made between 2003 and 2006 that led to a financial meltdown nationwide. What happens with these loans is that the initial payments are inexpensive because the borrower is basically just paying the interest on the loan, and not paying anything on the principal. After five years, the borrower is expected to begin paying on the principal and the payments balloon to unaffordable levels. At that point, the developer or bank can reclaim the house and begin the scheme all over again with another buyer. Wilkinson reports that the Blands' lawyer warned them about the financial trap and, forewarned, Bland was able to prepare for and escape the trauma of losing the property she had worked so hard to obtain. Eventually, when the children were grown and departed, the Blands purchased a lot, and then another "on contract," in Bethune Beach. However, it wasn't until 1977, decades after Bethune herself had passed, that they could afford to build a home there. The pace of individual lot sales and home building was simply too slow to sustain the whole.

During the last few years of her life, Bethune continued trying to turn Bethune Beach into a success. By the early 1950s, then in her late seventies, she pushed forward with building a motel and lounge near the property so those who visited for the day could stay overnight at Bethune Beach, as opposed to having to travel at night through areas of the county that were known to be unsafe for Black people. As was so often the case with projects she founded, financing remained an issue. Black people who invested initially could not always keep up the installment payments and lost their investments. In the summer of 1952, Bethune issued a public "S.O.S. Call—To the Negro Citizens of America pleading for help with satisfying the mortgage obligation and overall financial investment in Bethune Beach." Through a letter she published in Black newspapers across the country, she told Black America that "the Mortgage on the unsold portion of the property is now $89,000. It is held by a white financier.... If the property is to be saved for Negroes of our own and future generations, we must immediately satisfy this mortgage obligation." She added, "We have struggled valiantly to hold to this property, because of the difficulty that Negroes have in purchasing beach sites. We need cooperation and reinforcement from Negroes who have faith in the working and investing strength of our own people. We want Negroes to own and control this Beach subdivision."[16] Her call was left substantively unanswered. Today the majority of homeowners at Bethune Beach are white.

Mary McLeod Bethune midwifed American Beach as proof that Black ice was just as cold as anyone's, and she dreamed of Bethune Beach doing the same. These were two places that fit together pieces of a puzzle about Black wealth, peace, safety, and survival. They show how home and leisure dreams on the land of their ancestors could be foundational for Black survival via community, safety, relaxation, and peace. This was not a longing for a house to own or a mortgage to pay. This land longing was not an empty call to kneel on the altar of capitalism but an acknowledgment of the where and how of political stability and long-term strategy. Bethune believed these beaches were about a place to call home, about the soil of one's ancestors, about red clay earth squashed between toes, a humid cloak of air that settles gently and feels as familiar as a baby's smell to a mother. It is a call to return to community and to think hard about the uses of Black capital as a weapon against the exploitative possibilities of capitalism itself.

When I interviewed Dr. Cole about American Beach, she told me a story about her earliest ancestors in Florida that is not about Bethune but about family and land and slavery and economic exploitation and Black people in the United States that is either the beginning of this story or its end. I can't quite decide, but I believe it is a story worth telling. In a very real way, long before either A. L. Lewis or Mary M. Bethune knew that one or the other existed, their family histories connected them. Both grew up hearing stories about how their respective great-grandmothers were born free in Senegal. They had listened to the family-passed tales portioned like mouthfuls of water savored by those whose throats were too long parched. For their whole lives, they heard how their kinfolk had, on that distant continent, in that unknown nation, been African royalty, maybe princesses, before they became an undifferentiated mass known as slave.

A. L. Lewis's great-grandmother was named Anta Madjiguene Jai Peya Fall Ndiaye. She was born in 1793, a princess in the Wolof Kingdom that today we would call Senegal, and kidnapped in 1806 when she was thirteen. She survived the depravations and diseases of the middle passage, landed in Cuba, and was immediately put up for auction. That is how the forty-one-year-old Florida-based slave trader named Zephaniah Kingsley came to own her. By the time Anta arrived in Florida and first saw the Kingsley plantation, which sat about twenty minutes from where American Beach would one day sit, she was pregnant with his child. Anta was not the first child he had forced to his cabin during his slave voyages. Kingsley also maintained relationships with three other African women who acted as co-wives or concubines: Flora H., Sarah M., and Munsilna McGundo. Anta, by virtue of her first giving birth in the polygamous family, remained the lead wife, or matriarch. Historian Daniel Schafer, Anta's biographer, says she would have been familiar with the concepts of polygamy and marrying a slave master to acquire one's freedom. Visitors to the plantation were invited to a dinner table where Kingsley displayed his multiracial children with pride. He provided them with the best education he could afford and, given his many years living in postrevolutionary Haiti, where the mixed-race people of African descent constituted a leadership class, he considered his own children a shield from any potential racial uprising. In the coming years, Anta would have three more children with Kingsley before he freed her and their children, gifted her with ownership of six slaves of her own, and appointed her his plantation manager. As Schaefer has said of Anta, her body became his, her children became slaves, and her name became Anna.

Marriages between white plantation owners and African women were common in East Florida because the Spanish recognized a separate class of free people of color and encouraged slaves to purchase their freedom. Providing just a bit of insight into their union, during an 1842 interview with the American abolitionist Lydia Maria Child, Kingsley described Anta as "a fine, tall figure, black as jet, but very handsome." He said she was "very capable and could carry on all the affairs of the plantation in my absence, as well as I could myself. She was affectionate and faithful, and I could trust her." One year later, nearing the end of his life and worried about how "the law may consider my acknowledged wife" (they had never been officially married by church or state), Kingsley wrote a last will and testament that read, "She has always been respected as my wife and as such I acknowledge her, nor do I think that her truth, honor, integrity, moral conduct or good sense will lose in comparison with anyone." As an emancipated woman, slaveowner, and manager of her "husband's" plantation, Anta oversaw sixty slaves at Fort

George Island. Perhaps it was due to her tutelage that over a period of years, Kingsley continually bemoaned the fact that those he owned and referred to as slaves, increasingly refused to obey him, saying before long, "myself and the overseer became completely divested of all authority over the negroes." Of particular concern seemed to be an indication that infanticide became increasingly more common among the slave population at Fort George. Remarking that the growing insubordination of the laborers left the power relations at a crucial impasse, Kingsley noted in frustration that "severity had no effect; it only made it worse; and I really believe that, in several instances, sick children were allowed to die, because the parents thought conscientiously that it was meritorious to transfer their offspring from a miserable and wicked world to a happy country, where they were in hopes of soon joining them!"[17]

Though Kingsley favored the Spanish three-tier system of white landowners, Black slaves, and freed Blacks, the Florida Territorial Council, the governing body of the area before statehood in 1845, began to pass laws that forbade interracial marriage and free Black people or their biracial children from inheriting property. To avoid having his wives or children have their freedom or property rights challenged, given that the new white supremacist government exhibited what he termed a "spirit of intolerant prejudice," Kingsley sent his wives, children, and slaves to Haiti, where he pur-chased a large plantation and, because white people did not own property in the Black nation, put the land in his son's name. Though slavery was not allowed in Haiti, Kingsley brought his slaves with him, but as indentured servants who he promised would be allowed to earn their freedom in nine years' time. Freedom rarely found them. In the 1842 inter-view with Lydia Maria Child, she asked him if he was aware that his occupation as a slave trader might be perceived as being akin to piracy. He said he was aware and opined that when he was young, slavery was considered a respectable trade, adding, "The first merchants in England and America were engaged in it. Some people hide things which they think other people don't like. I never conceal anything."

Kingsley died in 1843 on his way to New York to work on a land deal. Anta returned to Florida in 1846 to defend her property rights when some of her husband's white relatives challenged her right to inherit his estate because she was Black and, under the laws in Florida, not legally eligible to own or inherit property. However, because the will had been made under Spanish law, according to which inheritance by free Blacks was legal, the court ruled in her favor, so control of the Kingsleys' holdings in Florida remained with her and her children for several years. Anta Kingsley remained in the United States after the trial concluded and became the matriarch of the surviving members of her family. She purchased a farm located between the plantation residences of her two daughters and helped found a free Black community on the eastern shore of the St. Johns River. In 1860, more than eighty "free persons of color" lived in the community, most of them Kingsley family members or their former slaves. The community survived until Florida seceded from the United States on the eve of the Civil War. Fearing life in the pro-slavery Confederate States of America, they sought safety in free states to the north. After the war ended in 1865, Anta Jai returned to Florida with her daughters Martha Baxter and Mary Sammis to what remained of their estates. Her wealth had vanished. In June 1870, Anta Madjiguene Jai Kingsley died. She was buried in a family cemetery near the house where her daughter Mary Sammis lived. Mary was Abraham Lincoln Lewis's wife and Johnnetta Cole's great-grandmother.

Land, violence, family, capital, property, community, and freedom mean the same things in different eras, even as the context for understanding how it all connects is necessary. Dead Africans, slave-owning Black women, a Black man named Abraham Lincoln, a Black woman who got a white president to donate land to start a Black beach. It all connects as imperfectly and incompletely as anything ever thought. What I think connects it all is understanding that the right to own land, to keep it once it is owned, to create community, to begin businesses, and to know peace are and always have been the perennial problems to which one generation after another of Black people in the United States has returned.

7

ON PEACE

A s she neared her seventh decade and gazed back over her life and assessed her work, Bethune could see that progress had taken place and that she had held a steadying hand on the wheel steering the way to Black survival. She had founded a school for Black girls that was by then coeducational and a fully accredited university. She had led on the issue of voting rights and the expansion of citizenship protections, and ensured that Black women and children were able to benefit from federal programs and opportunities. Her work was not done. She began to ponder what would come next. Her vision turned toward colonialism, anticolonialism, world peace, and the future of women around the globe. In her late seventies, afraid that she and her generation had been unable to move the needle sufficiently, Bethune struggled with the way to best tell a whole, full, contextual story about Black freedom and Black women's leadership in relation to it. That is how it came to be that near the end of her life, Bethune shifted her focus from the United States and its history with racism and segregation to institutions with worldwide reach. She began by planning the future of the United Nations.

According to Kim Cary Warren's rigorously researched article on Bethune's participation in the five-week conference that led to the founding of the United Nations, as Bethune made her way across the country, her private train suite was a magnet for the other attendees, such as NAACP president Walter White and activist and intellectual W. E. B. Du Bois as well as executives from the Black press, including those representing the *Chicago Defender*, where Bethune would a few years later write a monthly column. Bethune knew she had been invited to the conference to represent the NAACP; she was, after all, part of the administrative leadership, serving at the time as vice president. But she dearly wanted to register as a member of the organization for Black women that she had founded almost a decade before, the National Council of Negro Women. It was more than just an act of vanity; she hoped to be able to say that a group specifically representing Black women had a seat at that table. Choosing to ask for forgiveness as opposed to permission, though she had already been informed by the White House that she was there representing the NAACP, when Bethune arrived at the registration area, she insisted to the officials that the credentials they had for her saying she was a representative of the NAACP were in error. She told them she was there to represent the National Council of Negro Women. Told in no uncertain terms that the only Black organization of the forty-two groups authorized to officially participate was the NAACP and that if she was not there to represent them, she would have to leave, she finally acquiesced. In whatever capacity, Bethune was there to make clear in no uncertain terms that her view of the future enshrined the radical idea that Black people were human, Black women were women, and everyone, wherever they lived, deserved human rights.[1]

The registration process would not represent the end of the controversy for Bethune. Stories began to emerge from reporters covering the proceedings about how it was that Bethune had come to participate in the conference. First there were stories in the Black and white press about how Truman's secretary of state had originally wanted the group representing the United States at the international gathering to be all white. Given the outcry from civil rights organizations to the prospect of an all-white delegation, the president had relented and said members of the NAACP might attend, although initially he restricted the attendees to just Walter White and W. E. B. Du Bois. Bethune knew how to play politics very well, and given her contacts with influential Black newspapers such as the *Chicago Defender* and *The Pittsburgh Courier*, it is conceivable that she may have helped to plant some of these stories that created the uproar and gave her the opening to lobby to join the proceedings because of the ensuing public pressure. The personal entreaty from Eleanor Roosevelt did the trick. Once appointed, Bethune, White, and Du Bois developed a game plan aimed at convincing the US delegation to adopt a position denouncing colonialism and linking the oppression and exploitation of Black people in the United States to the denial of human rights for colonized people. The three agreed that their goal was to have the new body base its founding on the understanding that struggles for civil rights in the United States, anticolonialism, and human rights were intertwined. Thus, the three argued, as long as "Africans were subjected to white colonialism, African Americans stood little chance of overcoming white supremacy."[2]

With agreement as to their guiding principles, the Black delegates set to work, though they were not a united front. The degree of their disunity became clear the day before the formal start of the conference when White and Du Bois, without consulting or informing Bethune, issued a statement on behalf of the Black delegation about their rejection of colonialism, and urged the US delegation as a whole "to support the incorporation of clauses recognizing racial equality, an international bill of rights, and the abolition of colonialism." Upon learning that her colleagues had cut her out, Bethune was reportedly furious with them, claiming that neither man had asked her thoughts on the resolution. Fighting fire with fire, she held her own press conference without White and Du Bois where she reiterated her support for an international movement linking and rejecting colonization and racism.[3]

The tension between the Black delegates soon became a story in and of itself. *The New Journal and Guide* ran the headline "Bethune Rift Flares Anew in 'Frisco,'" telling readers, "The full inside story will have to be told later, but it is true that a schism has developed between Mrs. Bethune and the other two official Negro consultants." Another of the articles in the *Chicago Defender* about the gendered tension at the conference noted Bethune's efforts to use her position as head of the NCNW to make "contact with women of many minority groups and colored women of many countries," adding, "While it seems to be a 'MAN'S WORLD,' as men see it, thinking women are glad to know that a sprinkling of women will be—at least—nearby when 'MEN' attempt to make plans for the arbitration of world evils." The ill will be-tween the Black delegates was not confined by gender. In addition to standing with Du Bois in his effort to isolate Bethune, White also attempted to throw Du Bois under the bus when he privately criticized Du Bois and Bethune in a conversation with civil rights leader Roy Wilkinson. He made a point of mentioning that "Du Bois and Bethune haven't the stamina" to withstand the demands of the job. Unsurpris-ingly, as the weeks passed in San Francisco, Bethune further distanced herself from White, who had taken to chatting with anyone who cared to hear about his opinion of Bethune's attempt to register for the conference as a representative of the NCNW, rather than the NAACP.[4]

For her part, Bethune responded to both White and the anonymous calls for her to relinquish her post if she was not happy by making clear she believed the issue her male de-tractors really had was more about gender than it was per-sonal. She gave interviews in the Black press saying that if she did decide to resign her post in protest, they would still be unhappy as she would make sure to "give it to another woman." As the self-declared representative of all Black women, she turned the critiques of her actions into an op-portunity to amplify the larger issue with which she was concerned. She explained that she stood firmly in alliance with every other woman of color around the world, reasoning that this position "allowed black women to espouse a *majority* position in a society that had otherwise discounted their ideas as insignificant or only relevant to a minority of the population." Though ultimately leaving the conference disillusioned by her fellow Black delegates, and disappointed that the UN delegation unilaterally rejected the plea to denounce colonization and to see Black people in the United States as in need of protection and support from the international organization, Bethune would spend the rest of her life articulating a vision of a future world held together by an embrace of human rights for all, especially the millions of Black women around the world.

As she neared her eightieth year, it was time, Bethune decided, to take stock. She found another organization interested in the cause of Black freedom. When she was buried on the grounds of Bethune-Cookman University, the two symbols she wanted to have mark the spot were an elephant figurine to represent the Deltas, a Black women's sorority, and a figure of a bell, representing the Moral Re-Armament movement.[5]

A few years after the UN conference, Bethune had a type of spiritual reawakening as an invited guest at a conference of the World Assembly for Moral Re-Armament (MRA) in

Caux, Switzerland. It was a relationship so profound that she told an interviewer, "For four weeks I sat in those meetings and didn't think about my college or my country or my children or myself. I used the time to turn the searchlight on Mary McLeod Bethune." An international organization, the MRA had the goal of ushering in a new world order that was not based on capitalism, power, militarism, or inequality but on ethical principles and a commitment to peace. Converts vowed to uphold four absolutes: "Absolute Honesty, Absolute Purity, Absolute Unselfishness, and Absolute Love."[6]

According to historian Barbara Savage, when Bethune spoke at Caux, she struck a confessional tone, enumerating her "imperfections," which included putting her school before the needs of her son. As she surveyed the totality of the life she had lived and its accomplishments, and reflected on this new organization, she believed she had found something she had long been looking for. She said, "In Moral Re-Armament I have seen the nations of the world standing together regardless of race, class, or color. To be a part of this great uniting force of our age is the crowning experience of my life." The organization was started by an American minister named Frank Buchman in 1938 as fascism and militarism were tightening their grip on Europe. Buchman believed that military rearmament alone could not resolve the crisis because "the crisis is fundamentally a moral one. The nations must re-arm morally." Then-senator Harry Truman was a fan of the group, saying, "Where others have stood back and criticized, they have rolled up their sleeves and gone to work. They have already achieved remarkable results in bringing teamwork into industry, on the principles not of 'who's right' but of 'what's right.'" Buchman believed that if large groups practiced these principles in their own lives, they would be empowered to dismantle oppressive regimes, for example, in South Africa, where he was focusing some of his organizing.[7]

Buchman reached out to include Black people struggling for freedom around the globe, to try to draw them into his movement, offering Moral Re-Armament as an ideological alternative to communism and as a way to heal the hatreds of colonial oppression. Those were the claims that had first attracted Bethune to the MRA movement in the late 1930s and she later devoted several of her newspaper columns to the group and its work in South Africa, which had gained the support of the African National Congress.[8] Bethune spent two full weeks in Caux. When writing about the experience in her column for the *Chicago Defender*, she reflected, "As I sit 3,000 feet above sea level overlooking Lake Geneva, surrounded by the snow-capped Swiss and French Alps, at the World Assembly for Moral Re-Armament, my heart reaches out to all the readers of this column with a sincere desire that every single one of you might be as privileged as I am these days to sit with 800 from 30 nations gathered from all over the world." According to Savage, Bethune told all who would listen that the power of the gathering convinced her that MRA was the best and only way to achieve global peace, a way to end discrimination against people of color all over the world. In addition to writing about the group in her column, she took her enthusiasm for the movement to radio, telling an interviewer that her trip to Caux had been the "greatest experience of my life" and that it was "like opening a new door," where there was hope for improved race relations in the United States. She shared that she "could not help realizing as these men spoke that here was the spirit that could implement the recent legislation on segregation and make it work. Laws alone can never remove the hates and bitterness from the human heart."[9]

In her address to the assembly at Caux, Bethune went to great lengths to apologize publicly to her son, Albert, whose needs she believed she had neglected in pursuit of her work, her ambition, and her school. She told the assembled crowd, "I think first of my son, my only son, my only child," she said, "how I had to leave him in the care of others as I tramped all over America looking for nickels, dimes, dollars, and quarters," despite his repeated pleas to her not to leave him again. Although she rationalized that her work was for a broader good, she also regretted that her public commitments had blinded her to her son's emotional needs. As Barbara Savage has written about Bethune's relationship with MRA, it was in the privacy of her personal letters that Bethune expressed herself most passionately about her newfound belief in the movement, which preoccupied her in the final months of her life. In a letter to a colleague, Bethune explained how she had been affected by attending those meetings. "All of the assemblies were glorious. The peoples of the world were there. The silent hours, the testimonials, the listening for the guidance we need in all that we do are so enriching." Bethune also tried to bring attention to the group in other ways. She pleaded with Claude Barnett of the Black Newspapers Association to devote press coverage to the events sponsored by the organization, telling him, "The most important Assembly of our time is being held now at Mackinac Island under the auspices of Moral Re-Armament," and saying that the movement "has the answer to the conflicting problems of America and the world. Our public relations department would like to send you a daily coverage of what is going on here, so that the Negro people of America may know more definitely about the scope and importance of this Assembly." As Savage points out, some members of the Black press expressed skepticism about MRA, wondering if Bethune's ailing health and advanced age were clouding her judgment about the group.[10]

The group did have its detractors. While talking with Oprah Winfrey about her time growing up as a member of the MRA, the actress Glenn Close described the experience as growing up in a "cult" and said it had a supremely detrimental impact on her life. She talked about how her father, Dr. William Taliaferro Close, joined the Moral Re-Armament group when she was only seven and moved the family to the group's headquarters in Switzerland in 1954. Close remained in the MRA until she was fifteen, when she left Switzerland and moved to Virginia to pursue acting. Opening up about her experience with MRA, Close said, "Because of how we were raised, anything you thought you'd do for yourself was considered selfish." Bethune's speeches at Moral Re-Armament meetings hit somewhat upon this theme. She thought aloud about what it meant for her to have been a working mother and placing political and educational organizing and work ahead of raising Albert, in a lament that has long been true for many highly driven and successful women who are mothers.

In one such speech delivered at a meeting held in Mount Kisco, New York, she shared that she had been "on the fringe of Moral Re-Armament for the past 15 years" but had resisted getting "into the deep water." She said, "In America we have suffered so in segregation. You can't sleep here; you can't listen to music there; you can't do this; you can't do that." She added, "As I looked, I saw Frank Buchman with his army of men and women from all over the world touching one another, all God's children, all waiting for his voice to direct them, all banding together as one great army to go out to the world to preach justice." She felt that compared with this sense of a worldwide movement, her work had been too individualistic, too focused on "Mary McLeod Bethune."[11]

In these last few years, Bethune began to incorporate the language of Moral Re-Armament into explanations of her philosophy of life, whether she fully named it as such or not. When a young student wrote to her as part of a school project, asking about what constituted habits for good living, Bethune responded by calling upon MRA principles, saying, "The attributes that I am trying now day by day to keep alive in my daily life are absolute purity, absolute honesty, absolute unselfishness, absolute love. These are the standards and attributes of Moral Re-Armament—an ideology that will save the world from war and strife and will make us brothers the world over."[12] On another occasion, Bethune wrote to her longtime friend Charles S. Johnson, who was then president of Fisk University. She was almost evangelical in her testimony about how the movement had impacted her writing: "It has done so much for me, Charles. It has strengthened me spiritually. It has given me power. . . . I hope that it may become more vivid to you." She also urged Johnson and their colleague Horace Mann Bond, Lincoln University's president, to give an honorary degree to Buchman "as our stamp of approval of the great leadership that he is giving in this time when godly leaders are needed." It is not clear if Charles Johnson had a relationship with Buchman, but Horace Mann Bond, the father of Student Nonviolent Coordinating Committee (SNCC) activist and politician Julian Bond, did. He had asked Buchman for financial support when the Presbyterian Church withdrew funding for his school. Savage says Horace Mann Bond proposed that the MRA establish an institute at Lincoln devoted to the movement's principles and linked to the school's program in international reconciliation and education. The following year, Bond supported Buchman's nomination for a Nobel Peace Prize, citing MRA's "support for the work of two Lincoln alumni, prime ministers Kwame Nkrumah of Ghana and Nnamdi Azikiwe of Nigeria."[13]

Bond and Bethune were not the only prominent Black supporters of the organization. *Ebony* magazine devoted coverage to the MRA, focusing on its work in Africa. In addition, Vivian Mason, the woman who took over the leadership of the National Council of Negro Women after Bethune retired, was such a devout MRA follower that some complained that the group was distracting her from her duties as president of the NCNW. In addition to members of the NCNW becoming devoted to the group, the same was true for the National Association of Colored Women's Clubs, which, years after Bethune's death, gave Buchman an award in 1958. There were also several other Black public figures deeply impacted by the group's message of reconciliation and forgiveness. This included Daisy Bates, an Arkansas journalist and NAACP leader who is best remembered for her leadership role in working to desegregate Little Rock's Central High School. Bates said the movement's tenets lifted "a hatred of whites from her heart."[14]

In 1955, during one of her last talks at Bethune-Cookman, Bethune advocated for a meditation center to be built on the campus, saying to the assembled crowd, "Young people, begin now to give a special portion of the day to meditation, so that your spiritual lives may be fed and your soul enriched and the fruit of your lives multiplied through your sincere devotion to what is highest and best. May every one of you join with me as I strive daily toward absolute purity, absolute honesty, absolute unselfishness, absolute love through God's guidance."

The MRA movement became her guiding principle in life. Looking at where she began, and comparing it with where she ended, her political strategizing and thinking surely changed. When Bethune first hit the political scene as a school founder, organizer, and champion of organizations, she had grounded her theory of change on the belief in a pure, unfettered, and antiracist embrace of democratic principles and of governmental change that would include Black people. By 1945, she was less sure about the path ahead even as she continued to believe that organizing and strength in numbers was still the surest way forward. As a delegate to the UN Charter meeting, Bethune made concrete her thinking that Black women should ally themselves with Black women and other women of color around the globe. She began to envision freedom in terms that were both more international and more integrated, even as she regretted what her political visions and ambitions had cost her personally.

As Bethune reflected on how to balance work, ideology, money, and fame with a family and home life, she realized her commitments may have interfered with her family relationships. She came to understand that the costs, though perhaps unavoidable, may have been higher and more deeply felt than she had initially thought. I don't know if it was worth it to her. Selfishly, I am inspired by so many aspects of her life and legacy that I find it hard to imagine her taking her foot off the gas, if even just a little bit. What she did, thought, dared, and imagined inspires me. I think she should inspire us all.

I look at images when I write. There is one I have stared at often while thinking about the last few years of Mary McLeod Bethune's life and political evolution. I moved it from a spot behind me when I first began the project and hung it on a wall at eye height as I came to the end of this book. It is a photograph of what looks to be a teenage Black girl tugging on one end of a pole with an American flag on the other end of it. She's in a pink hoodie and the muscles in her neck strain with the effort of holding and pulling as she has rocked back on her heels so far, if there were a chair behind her, she could almost sit in it. The other figure in the photograph, holding on to the end of the pole set closer to the flag, is an adult white man. He towers over the young woman in the pink hoodie, and his mouth locked into a resolute line sneers down at her. Because the top of the pole with the flag is nearest to him, he literally has the upper hand, is advantaged by his size and strength, but also by his position in this struggle. Though the young woman is pulling with her whole body, and it is a one-on-one contest, his size, leverage, and positioning make it seem clear that he will win the contest.

This moment was captured outside Rams Stadium in St. Louis in October 2014, by a photographer named David

Carson, who snapped a series of images of this battle for the flag. He won a Pulitzer for it and sixteen other photographs he made documenting the Black Lives Matter protests that took place in Ferguson, Missouri, that year. The blurb under the headline as it appeared in the *St. Louis Post-Dispatch* read: "Protesters fight to regain control of a flag that was taken by a fan. Two women were arrested after dozens of Rams fans and Ferguson protesters clashed. A scuffle broke out when fans argued with the protesters who had been yelling and chanting about the killing of Michael Brown, a black 18-year-old, who was shot by a police officer."[15] The caption was striking to me because most of the context for the image took place outside the frame. Its accompanying article was not about how an adult who disagreed with the politics of the moment and with the young woman holding on to an American flag during a protest determined that he would take it from her by force. Also, other than mentioning that the police had arrested "two women," this particular young woman was not immediately identified. As it turns out, just a little bit of research turned up her name, Cheyanne Green, and she was eighteen when the image was made. At the time, she had recently cofounded an organization in Ferguson named Lost Voices. It didn't take long to find out more about her, to give her a history and context. Even before I started looking for her, for the specifics and particulars of her life, I was taken with the image of her fighting to hold on to what was hers, be it her property, her rights to protest, her citizenship. What *I* saw in that image was her back-straightening act of heroic individualism. A lone Black woman standing up to a much larger white man who was trying to take from her what was hers, or maybe ours. She could be Rosa, or Harriet, or any individual one of us who will / have to / does resist the theft of our identity, our community, our bodies, our spirits, our being.

Then I saw a second image. It shows what happened a few minutes later and a whole other side of publicly circulated images of Black women and girls. In this one, two Black women, one older than the other, appear to be hitting a defenseless white man over the head with a flag attached to a pole. When asked by a writer from *Ebony* magazine what was going on that day, the mother of the young woman told the full story of both photographs in the moments between the first image being snapped and the second one. She said the man in both photographs "*hog*-spit at my baby. He *hog*-spit. He took everything out of him and spit in my daughter's face. She is a minor. That's the absolute worst thing you can do, when you spit on another human being. She was just saying 'No justice, no peace' and he hog-spit (at) and then smacked my baby. At that time—there was no more being peaceful."

Police arrested the mother, Tiny, and her daughter, Dasha,

and charged them with two felony counts each. None of the white protesters was even questioned or detained. Spitting, the mother and daughter learned that day, is not considered assault. Disrespect is not a prosecutable offense. Tiny said, "We shouldn't have to feel this way." That day, spitting and disrespect further radicalized nineteen-year-old Dasha, who was also a member of Lost Voices. When asked about what she had seen as she watched, she said, "I saw the true colors of our country today. There's still so much racism. And it's going to take a minute, but me, I know I'm going to get it done."[16]

For me this image encapsulates much about how and why the spirit of Bethune matters today. It is not because we somehow have no freedom fighters without her. This image shows us this is not the case. It is because Bethune's faith in the power of Black girls and women to stand up and fight for change is exemplified here. It is an image that clarifies what it means to begin from a place of believing that it is possible for Black women and girls to "get it done." Bethune's thinking, development, and strategizing provide a road map so that each generation does not have to keep re-creating the map from scratch. The truths of one century and generation connect with those of the next in understanding that it is never okay for spit of either the metaphorical or the actual variety to drip off the face of a Black teenager. That can never be the end of a story. So many of the images and pictures we have of Black women and girls in this country are at best partial truths with a contextualizing story that we must look for—or find a way to let Black women and girls tell the story for themselves. Bethune taught me that there is strength in numbers, always a reason to hope, and that if someone disrespects you and yours, it is in your best interest to find a way to use the metaphorical flag that professes your citizenship, rights, and humanity as a weapon, and "get it done." These are Bethune's truths. This was Bethune's life.

ACKNOWLEDGMENTS

There would be no book without my agent, Tanya McKinnon. I wasn't planning to write a book about Mary McLeod Bethune until she asked me one day, out of the blue, after a rushed "hello," whom I would write about if I could write about anyone I wanted. I blurted out something or other at her question. I was like a game-show contestant hurling an answer in response when they are fully sure of neither the question nor the answer. I don't remember whom I first said I wanted to write about, but when Tanya asked me who else, I just took a breath and let come whatever wanted to flow forth. I said I wanted to write about Bethune. I hadn't known it until I heard the answer, but I immediately knew it was true. Tanya is intuitive like that, and supportive like that, and honest like that, and she made me know I could take this on and made me believe that I could do it justice.

There would be no book without the relatively small but uniformly brilliant, insightful, and rigorous group of scholars who have unearthed so much of who Bethune was and worked hard to keep her memory relevant. They are Audrey Thomas McCluskey, Johnnetta Cole, Jenny Woodley, Elaine Smith, Joyce Hanson, Barbara Savage, Ashley Robertson, and Martha Jones.

There would be no book without my editors at Penguin Press, Skip Gates and Scott Moyers. They gave me the opportunity to immerse myself in Bethune and then were patient and kind with me and my writing as I careened around, trying to figure out what I wanted to say, and how to say it.

There would be no book without the music of Frankie Beverly and Maze, who carried me the last mile of the way.

There would be no book without my life partner, Bill Gaskins, who, after twenty-five years, still teaches me the how, why, and ways of love on the regular.

NOTES

1. "MY NAME IS MRS. BETHUNE"

1. Jeremy Gray, "In 1938 Birmingham, Eleanor Roosevelt Faced Bull Connor's Wrath," AL.com, April 24, 2019, https://www.al.com/news/2019/04/in-1938-birmingham-eleanor-roosevelt-defied-bull-connor.html.

2. Interview with Virginia Foster Durr, October 16, 1975, Interview G-0023-3, Southern Oral History Program Collection (#4007) in the Southern Oral History Program Collection, Southern Historical Collection, Wilson Library, University of North Carolina at Chapel Hill.

3. Jerry Marx, "Mary McLeod Bethune (1875–1955)—Educator, Public Administrator, and Civil Rights Activist," Social Welfare History Project (2011), retrieved July 31, 2022, https://socialwelfare.library.vcu.edu/people/bethune-mary-mcleod/.

4. Henry Louis Gates, "Three Women 'Red Tails' Left Out of Its Story," *The Bay State Banner,* February 1, 2012, https://www.baystatebanner.com/2012/02/01/three-women-red-tails-left-out-of-its-story/.

5. Mito Habe-Evans, "Eleanor Roosevelt's Flight with the First Black Aviators," NPR, *The Picture Show,* March 25, 2011, https://www.npr.org/sections/pictureshow/2011/03/25/134769323/black_aviators.

6. Audrey Thomas McCluskey, "Ringing Up a School: Mary McLeod

Bethune's Impact on Daytona," *The Florida Historical Quarterly* 73, no. 2 (October 1994): 61.

7. Deborah Gray White, *Too Heavy a Load: Black Women in Defense of Themselves* (New York: W. W. Norton, 1999), 152–55.

8. Paul Ortiz, *Emancipation Betrayed: The Hidden History of Black Organizing and White Violence in Florida from Reconstruction to the Bloody Election of 1920* (Berkeley: University of California Press, 2005), 194.

9. Ashley N. Robertson, *Mary McLeod Bethune in Florida: Bringing Social Justice to the Sunshine State* (Charleston, SC: The History Press, June 29, 2015), 38.

10. James C. Clark, "Lynching: Florida's Brutal Distinction," *Orlando Sentinel*, March 7, 1993, https://www.orlandosentinel.com/news/os-xpm -1993-03-07-9303070156-story.html.

11. Matt Grimson, "Historically Black Beach Disappears with Integration," *Naples Daily News,* October 13, 2003.

12. Audrey Thomas McCluskey and Elaine M. Smith (eds.), *Mary McLeod Bethune: Building a Better World, Essays and Selected Documents* (Bloomington: Indiana University Press, 1999), 69.

13. Elaine Smith, "Introduction," *Mary McLeod Bethune Papers: The Bethune-Cookman College Collection, 1922–1955,* Black Studies Research Sources microfilm project (Bethesda, MD: University Publications of America, 1995).

14. Barbara Savage, *Your Spirits Walk beside Us: The Politics of Black Religion* (Cambridge, MA: Belknap Press, 2012), 151–60.

2. REMEMBERING BETHUNE

1. Jackie Johnson, "Mary McLeod Bethune," South Carolina Hall of Fame, February 20, 2020, https://www.scetv.org/stories/2020/mary -mcleod-bethune-sc-hall-fame.

2. "The Extraordinary Life of Mary McLeod Bethune," The National World War II Museum, July 30, 2020, https://www.nationalww2mu seum.org/war/articles/mary-mcleod-bethune.

3. "The Mary McLeod Bethune Trail," US National Park Service, https:// dokumen.tips/documents/the-mary-mcleod-bethune-trail-national -park-service-mary-mcleod-bethune-was-born.html?page=2.

3. MEETING BETHUNE

1. Patricia and Fredrick McKissack, *Mary McLeod Bethune: A Great Teacher* (Berkeley Heights, NJ: Enslow Publishers, 2001), 19.
2. Eileen Zaffiro-Kean, "A Saint and a Special Person: New Mary McLeod Bethune Statue to Be Unveiled in Daytona Beach," *The Daytona Beach News-Journal*, October 10, 2021, https://www.news-journalonline.com/story/news/2021/10/10/daytona-beach-will-host-the-new-marble-mary-mcleod-bethune-statue/5986207001/.
3. David Silkenat, *Raising the White Flag: How Surrender Defined the American Civil War* (Chapel Hill: University of North Carolina Press, April 2019), 253–61.
4. Silkenat, 253–61.
5. Brian Palmer and Seth Freed Wessler, "The Costs of the Confederacy," *Smithsonian Magazine*, December 2018, https://www.smithsonianmag.com/history/costs-confederacy-special-report-180970731/.
6. Allison Parker, "When White Women Wanted a Monument to Black 'Mammies,'" *The New York Times,* February 6, 2020, https://www.nytimes.com/2020/02/06/opinion/sunday/confederate-monuments-mammy.html.
7. Evolve Editorial Team, "The People's Choice: Mary McLeod Bethune Gets Statewide Support for Place in National Statuary Hall," *Parent Magazines Florida*, 2021, https://www.parentmagazinesflorida.com/2021/09/30/the-peoples-choice/.
8. "Capitol Hill Parks—Lincoln Park," US National Park Service, https://www.nps.gov/cahi/learn/historyculture/cahi_lincoln.htm.
9. Frederick Douglass, "1876 Speech Given by Frederick Douglass at the Unveiling of the Freedmen's Monument in Lincoln Park, Washington, DC," Digital Public Library of America, https://dp.la/primary-source-sets/frederick-douglass-and-abraham-lincoln/sources/104.
10. Alexandria Russell, "Sites Seen and Unseen: Mapping African American Women's Public Memorialization" (PhD diss., University of South Carolina, 2018), https://scholarcommons.sc.edu/cgi/viewcontent.cgi?article=6001&context=etd.
11. Jenny Woodley, "'Ma Is in the Park': Memory, Identity, and the Bethune Memorial," *Journal of American Studies* 52, no. 2 (2017): 17–20.

12. Woodley, 17–20.
13. "Bethune Memorial Is First Black Statue in the U.S. Capitol," *Jet*, August 1, 1974, 12.
14. Woodley, 21–22.
15. Woodley, 21–22.
16. Woodley, 21–22.
17. Mary McLeod Bethune, "My Last Will and Testament," *Ebony*, August 1955, https://radar.auctr.edu/islandora/object/auc.098%3A1091.
18. Jacob Ogles, "Lake County No Longer Wants Confederate Statue," *Florida Politics*, June 17, 2020, https://floridapolitics.com/archives/341431-lake-county-no-longer-wants-confederate-statue/.

4. "YOURS FOR NEGRO WOMANHOOD"

1. Audrey Thomas McCluskey, "Ringing Up a School: Mary McLeod Bethune's Impact on Daytona," *The Florida Historical Quarterly* 73, no. 2 (October 1994): 210–12.
2. McCluskey, 210–12.
3. Mary McLeod Bethune, "Memoir of Mary McLeod Bethune," in *Mary McLeod Bethune: Building a Better World* (Bloomington: Indiana University Press, 1999), 25.
4. Audrey Thomas McCluskey and Elaine M. Smith (eds.), *Mary McLeod Bethune: Building a Better World, Essays and Selected Documents* (Bloomington: Indiana University Press, 1999), 55.
5. Holley Snaith, "The First Lady of Struggle: The Remarkable Mary McLeod Bethune," *Medium*, February 5, 2022, https://medium.com/frame-of-reference/why-mary-mcleod-bethune-is-the-first-lady-of-the-struggle-d0f01752771d.
6. Rackham Holt, *Mary McLeod Bethune: A Biography—a Life Devoted to the Cause of Racial Equality* (New York: Doubleday, 1964), 106.
7. Joyce A. Hanson, *Mary McLeod Bethune and Black Women's Political Activism* (Columbia: University of Missouri Press, 2003), 104, http://ebookcentral.proquest.com/lib/brown/detail.action?docID=3570755.
8. Noliwe Rooks, *Ladies' Pages: African American Women's Magazines and the Culture That Made Them* (New Brunswick, NJ: Rutgers University Press, 2004), 50.

9. Hanson, 107.
10. Deborah Gray White, *Too Heavy a Load: Black Women in Defense of Themselves* (New York: W. W. Norton, 1999), 155.
11. McCluskey and Smith, 161.
12. McCluskey and Smith, 161.
13. Hanson, 160.
14. Hanson, 169.
15. Hanson, 170.
16. Hanson, 170.
17. Hanson, 170.
18. Hanson, 170.
19. Hanson, 171.

5. BLACK: CAPITAL, CAPITALISM, AND RELAXATION

1. Russ Rymer, *American Beach: A Saga of Race, Wealth, and Memory* (New York: HarperCollins, 1998), 69.
2. AP, "Five Drown in Florida Riptides," *The New York Times*, May 31, 1994, https://www.nytimes.com/1994/06/01/us/5-swimmers-are-drowned-in-a-riptide.html.
3. "Lesson in Survival: The Dark Yet Inspiring History of American Beach," *Culture Crush,* accessed July 23, 2022, https://www.theculture crush.com/insights/lesson-in-survival.
4. "The Middle Passage," US National Park Service, https://www.nps.gov/afbg/learn/historyculture/upload/FINALMiddlePassage.pdf.

6. ON THE SOIL AND IN THE NAME OF ONE'S ANCESTORS

1. "The Isle of Eight Flags," City of Fenandina Beach, Florida, https://www.fbfl.us/190/Isle-of-Eight-Flags.
2. DeNeen L. Brown, "40 Acres and a Mule: How the First Reparations for Slavery Ended in Betrayal," *The Washington Post*, April 15, 2021, https://www.washingtonpost.com/history/2021/04/15/40-acres-mule-slavery-reparations/.
3. Francis Wilkinson, "The Forgotten History of America's Black Beach Resorts: What Happened to the Vacation Spots Created by and for

Black Americans in the Mid-20th Century," Opinion, *Bloomberg News*, August 8, 2021, https://www.bloomberg.com/opinion/articles/2021 -08-08/the-forgotten-history-of-america-s-black-beach-resorts.

4. Russ Rymer, *American Beach: A Saga of Race, Wealth, and Memory* (New York: HarperCollins, 1998), 114–15.

5. Rymer, 169.

6. Johnnetta Cole, interview conducted by Noliwe Rooks, April 20, 2022.

7. Cole interview.

8. Rackham Holt, *Mary McLeod Bethune: A Biography—a Life Devoted to the Cause of Racial Equality* (New York: Doubleday, 1964), 150.

9. Wilkinson, "The Forgotten History of America's Black Beach Resorts."

10. Ethel Cook-Wilson, *Isn't That God's Water?: The Advent and Demise of Bethune-Volusia Beach Incorporated* (CreateSpace Independent Publishing Platform, 2015), 65–68.

11. Emily Keck, "Volusia County History: Racial Terror and Black Resilience," *Story Maps*, https://storymaps.arcgis.com/stories/6d8eb5ab fecb43488d95028240c72276.

12. Keck, "Volusia County History."

13. Mark Lane, "80 Years Ago a Lynching Prosecution Fell Apart," *The Daytona Beach News-Journal*, April 30, 2019, https://www.news -journalonline.com/story/opinion/columns/guest/2019/04/30/mark -lane-80-years-ago-lynching-prosecution-fell-apart/5298823007/.

14. Matt Grimson, "Historically Black Beach Disappears with Integration," *Naples Daily News*, October 13, 2003.

15. Cook-Wilson, *Isn't That God's Water?*, 85.

16. Mary McLeod Bethune, "Dr. Bethune Makes Plea to Citizens of America," *Miami Times*, July 26, 1952, https://chroniclingamerica.loc.gov /data/batches/fu_armadillo_ver01/data/sn83004231/00414180899 /1952072601/0437.pdf.

17. Vincent Brown, *The Reaper's Garden: Death and Power in the World of Atlantic Slavery* (Cambridge, MA: Harvard University Press, 2008), 248–49.

7. ON PEACE

1. Kim Cary Warren, "Mary McLeod Bethune's Feminism: Black Women as Citizens of the World," *Gender & History* 35, no. 1 (March 2023; first published August 24, 2021): 323–39, https://onlinelibrary.wiley.com /doi/10.1111/1468-0424.12556.

2. Carol Anderson, "From Hope to Disillusion: African Americans, the United Nations, and the Struggle for Human Rights, 1944–1947," *Diplomatic History* 20, no. 4 (Fall 1996): 535, https://academic.oup.com /dh/article-abstract/20/4/531/378883.

3. Anderson, 534.

4. Anderson, 534.

5. Yvonne Ryan, *Roy Wilkins: The Quiet Revolutionary and the NAACP* (Lexington: University Press of Kentucky, 2014), 36. For more on Bethune's relationship with the Black press, see Audrey Thomas McCluskey, "Representing the Race: Mary McLeod Bethune and the Press in the Jim Crow Era," *Western Journal of Black Studies* 23, no. 4 (Winter 1999): 236–45.

6. Audrey Thomas McCluskey and Elaine M. Smith (eds.), *Mary McLeod Bethune: Building a Better World, Essays and Selected Documents* (Bloomington: Indiana University Press, 1999), 33.

7. Fr. John A. Hardon, S.J., "An Evaluation of Moral Rearmament," The Real Presence Association, http://www.therealpresence.org/archives /Heresies_Heretics/Heresies_Heretics_008.htm.

8. Garth Mason, "The Moral Rearmament Activist: P.Q. Vundla's Community Bridge-Building during the Boycotts on the Witwatersrand in the Mid-1950s," *Journal for the Study of Religion* 28, no. 2 (2015): 154–80, http://www.jstor.org/stable/24805696.

9. Mary McLeod Bethune, "Hope of Africa Not in Revolution, but a New Dimension Free from Hate," *Chicago Defender*, April 3, 1954; Bethune, "Moral Re-Armament Movement Heavily Felt in Africa," *Chicago Defender,* April 24, 1954.

10. Barbara Savage, *Your Spirits Walk beside Us: The Politics of Black Religion* (Cambridge, MA: Belknap Press, 2012), 154–56.

11. Mary McLeod Bethune, "Transcript of Remarks," Dellwood, Mount

Kisco, New York, July 30, 1954, Moral Re-Armament Papers, Library of Congress.

12. Savage, 154.
13. Savage, 157.
14. Savage, 157.
15. Samantha Liss, "Police Arrest Two Ferguson Protesters in Clash with Rams Fans," *St. Louis Post-Dispatch*, October 20, 2014, https://www.stltoday.com/news/local/police-arrest-two-ferguson-protesters-in-clash-with-rams-fans/article_dcca3100-aa78-5ea0-a55f-c8833a07a4f6.html.
16. Warren, 323–39.

INDEX

INDEX